THE BLINDFOLDED M

Creation versus Destruction:
The power of economic networks

MICHAEL BAXTER

The Blindfolded Masochist
Creation versus Destruction: The power of economic networks

©Michael Baxter

ISBN: 978-1-906316-95-2

Published in 2011 by HotHive Books, Evesham, UK.
www.thehothive.com

A CIP record of this book is available from the British Library.

Printed in the UK by Jellyfish Print Solutions, Swanmore

CONTENTS

ABOUT THE AUTHOR

Michael Baxter's somewhat quirky writing, in combination with his take on the economy, has been drawing a wide audience for several years. He launched the daily newsletter *Investment and Business News* back in 2003, drawing rave feedback from readers and growing steadily in popularity. At the tail-end of 2006 it was sold to a well-known company in the financial services sector, with Michael continuing to write the newsletter editorial. Today his views on the economy are frequently quoted in the media. You can read his daily ponderings at http://www. share.com/a/archive-thought-for-the-day.html, you can follow him on Twitter @IABN_Newsflash, and see other articles he has produced at www.investmentandbusinessnews.co.uk

A prolific writer, Michael often produces several pieces numbering three or four thousand words a day. He focuses on trying to make his writing both entertaining and thought provoking, punctuated with the odd and occasionally funny joke.

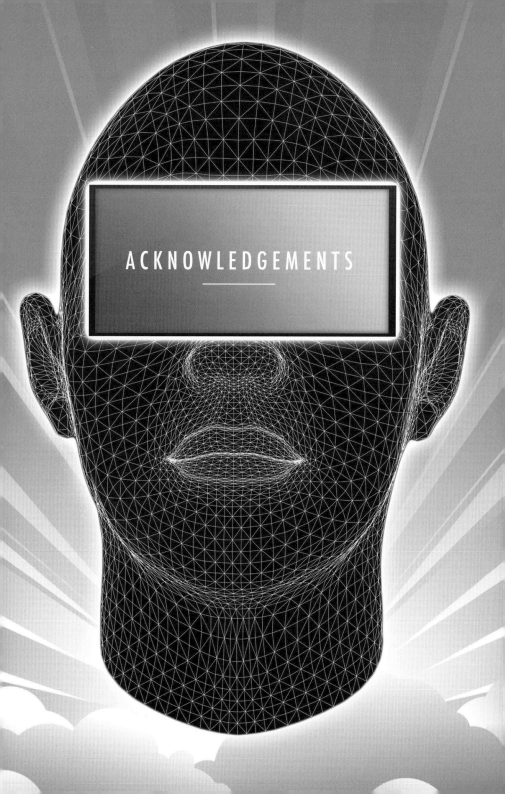

ACKNOWLEDGEMENTS

ACKNOWLEDGEMENTS

Beethoven composed his Ninth Symphony when he was deaf. It's considered by some, including me, one of the greatest pieces of music ever written. What is truly remarkable is how Beethoven created this piece in his mind, imagining the sound despite never being able to hear it. One of the key propositions of this book is that we are all influenced by others, no one is an island, no great idea is developed in isolation. Beethoven himself was a child of his time. Without Mozart, Beethoven's music would have been different. Perhaps it would never have existed. Inasmuch as his famous Choral Symphony built on Beethoven's past experiences then this piece too was a product of its time. However, that last hurdle, the one that took Beethoven from his eighth to his ultimate work, took place entirely in his head, in relative seclusion. As such, that beautiful piece of music is, in part, an exception to the rule.

This book is certainly no such exception. In producing it, I drew upon what I had learnt over the past few years. As such all those who helped me make *Investment and Business News* the product it became deserve my thanks. So that includes, among others, Peter Blenkinsop and Ian Speller who helped me get the newsletter off the ground, Steve George, for being my first investor and Alec O'Donnell who helped beef up my writing, and never let my brain rest. My wife Debbie deserves my thanks too, for more reasons than I might divulge here, but in one respect particularly, for it was she who told me to preserve my unusual sense of humour in my writing.

Not least, the many thousands of readers of my newsletter deserve my thanks. Without their praise, I would not have had the drive to continue to fight the good fight. During my time at Defaqto Brian Brown was always happy to debate economics, Kenn Herskind helped me see a wider perspective and Michael Allmey was a great help, proofing my writings and with an attention to detail I had never previously encountered. Kenn also worked with me on my previous book, *Bubbles and Wisdom*. Our early brainstorming sessions encouraged me to wider reading.

For *The Blindfolded Masochist*, I owe gratitude to Alec O'Donnell and Charles East, both of whom were more than happy to question my assumptions. Alec, in particular, threw himself into the book, and his efforts have proved to be essential. Above all, I would like to thank those blindfolded nodes out there in the network who have created our masochistic economy. If there was no such things as madness of crowds, and group polarisation, and banking crises such as the one we saw in 2008, the world we live in today might be a step closer to nirvana, but alas there would have been no need for this book.

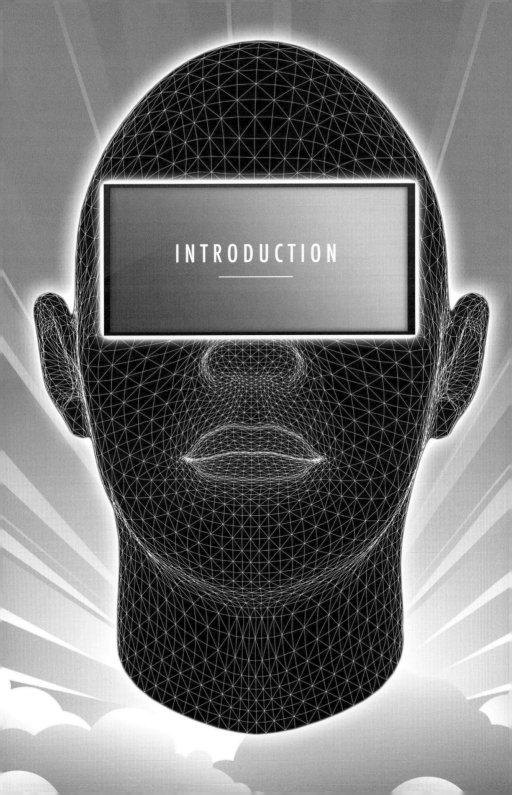

INTRODUCTION

INTRODUCTION

In March of 2011, a massive shoal of sardines was navigating through the Pacific Ocean just south of Los Angeles. They swam in tight formation, moving as one; to the observer, the shoal seemed to possess a collective intelligence. This particular group navigated their way into Redondo Beach's King Harbor, California. Apparently hell-bent on self-destruction, they failed to reverse course: caught in a trap of their own creation, they sucked the oxygen supply from the shallow waters, suffocating en masse.

This is an example of a network. Networks are everywhere. Fish, neurons, humans, computer servers: they can be made of anything. Such networks are brilliant indeed; they are also destructive. Their tendency for wanton self-inflicted damage can only be described as masochistic. The individual elements that form a network are neither aware of this tendency nor of the role they play in forming it; they wear a blindfold.

Local experts were not sure how the sardines had managed such a calamitous error. *The Guardian* reported on the incident, quoting Andrew Hughan, a spokesman from the California Department of Fish and Game. He told Reuters: "It looks like they just swam in the wrong direction and ended up in a corner of the pier that doesn't have any free-flowing oxygen in it. There's nothing that appears to be out of sorts, no oil sheen, no chemicals, no sign of any kind of illegal activity. As one fisherman just told me, this is natural selection." Hughan went on to say that such incidents were rare but not unheard of. He was not wrong in that respect. Just a few weeks later, another shoal off the California coast swam into Ventura Harbor; once again the over-concentration of fish swiftly exhausted the oxygen supply. They died, leaving the harbour patrol with the unpleasant job of clearing up.

Various theories have been proposed as to why the sardines adopted such short-sighted behaviour. One explanation put forward is that they were running from a "red tide": a bloom of marine algae that causes poison-related disorientation. Others proposed that the shoal was seeking refuge from an offshore storm. However, such explanations are not necessary.

Networks are quite capable of self-destruction; the behaviour of the sardines can be explained without recourse either to inclement weather, or to bad algae. Such is the nature of a network: whilst it appears to possess intelligence, it does not; if it did, such self-inflicted harm would surely be of no purpose.

The network that dragged the global economy to its knees, swimming the uncharted waters of financial toxicity was equally destructive. The individuals that constituted this network: bankers, regulators, economists and commentators were clearly lacking in vision. Just like the sardines, while their behaviour seemed appropriate on an individual basis, their collective actions were disastrous.

These bankers had come up with a cunning way of reducing their own individual risk when providing loans. The loans they made were re-packaged, chopped into little pieces and sold on. By dividing them up, if a given loan went bad, only a small percentage of the resulting loss would be felt by any one institution. They called it "mortgage securitisation". The financial network as a whole was lauded for its intelligence, for its creativity. So compelling was this new way of doing things that the IMF itself stated, in 2006, that the risk of a banking crisis had been reduced as a result. This claim was made a mere 18 months before the most serious financial meltdown of our times.[1]

The core of the problem was that on an individual loan by loan basis, this strategy made perfect sense. However, the mechanism proved to be catastrophic when applied across the economy as a whole. Because loans had been securitised, banks were no longer fully liable for the decisions they made: they began to provide more risky loans. Each bank mimicked the next to the extent that the entire banking system found itself exposed to an unsustainable asset bubble of its own creation. What the banks and the IMF failed to comprehend is that networks are dangerous: when crowds act in unison, when they engage in collective behaviour, their actions magnify systemic risk. Yet, the brilliance of the crowd and the power of the network can be quite incredible.

Us: that's you, me, the bloke next door and all of the members of *Homo sapiens sapiens*, are experts at working, playing, laughing and crying within our network. The product of our collective behaviour has enabled us

---

[1] *The influence of credit derivative and structured credit markets on financial stability* – Chapter II

to organise the world, create wonderful art and music, tame nature, and, most importantly, develop the potential to create unprecedented wealth and guarantee a prosperous future for each and every member of our species. In order to fulfil this potential, we must learn to see clearly, to understand the collective to which we belong, and in the process avoid the fate of the sardines of King Harbor. Unlike the bankers, we must avoid shallow economic waters; we must never deprive ourselves of the oxygen that gives life to the global economy and indeed, our global civilisation.

First of all, however, we need to have a better understanding of networks. Network theory is a relatively new area of study, but it is shining light on mysteries that have long been a source of puzzlement. To use the jargon, the individual components that make up a network are nodes and the way they connect with each other is crucial. Some nodes are highly connected: these are the hubs of the network. The network's structure and emergent properties, where chaos at the local level creates order at the group level, is the stuff of magic.

To fully realise how the human network operates, we must learn of our evolution and the inherent failings of our minds, our tendencies as individuals and our society as a whole. As individuals within the network we are simply one of the many nodes in the system, one of the particles in the chaos. The greatest figures of history do nothing more than fulfil the role that the network demands of them; they are dust in the wind, grist to the mill. As a crowd, we are both brilliant and frightening. Our capability for innovation, for discovery and achievement are awesome: in the mere few millennia of our history as a species, we have changed the world more completely than it has changed us. Yet, given our abilities, our history is littered with events that we were able to prevent: wars that did not need to be fought, famines we could have prevented, oppression that should never be tolerated and ignorance both wilful and shameful.

The crowd is a genius – and a madman.

Today we have new hope; we possess the tools, the skills and the means to overcome all of that. We have the ability to take humanity into a new and golden age, to learn from the mistakes of history, to avoid the pitfalls of our evolution and psychology, to put an end to the harm we inflict upon ourselves. We can harness the power of our network and make it work for us. There are few challenges more important than these.

CHAPTER 1

Networks and Network Theory

Part I – Theories

CHAPTER 1

Networks and Network Theory

The princess arrives at a state banquet, stunning in a beautiful dress, tiara, necklace, bracelet and rings. Her adornments are not studded with twinkling stones, as one might expect. To the consternation of the onlookers, the guests, servants and her jeweller, she has had them decorated with coal. The people stare at her, incredulous. Coal!

Networks are More Than the Sum of Their Parts

The individual units that make up a network, which in network theory are known as "nodes" or "vertices", are not themselves responsible for its features and capabilities. The connections between the nodes have far more impact on the network than the nodes themselves.

If our princess had chosen rubies or sapphires instead of diamonds then her fashion choice would have been of no great moment. However, the chemical difference would have been far more substantial. For, at the atomic level, diamonds and coal are made of the same thing: carbon. The difference lies in the network formed by their constituent atoms. To use network terminology, the nodes are the same, but the connections between them determine whether the structure is one of a precious stone, or a dirty black rock useful only as fuel.

That's the point. A network is not defined by its nodes, but by the structure of the connections between them.

The same principle also determines the difference between water vapour, liquid water and ice. In ice, water molecules are packed in tight, neat formations. In liquid, the network is less structured. In water vapour, the connections between molecules are highly dynamic. It could be said that in ice, the water molecules are trapped, unable to move, but in vapour they have freedom.

It is estimated that most, if not all, of the atoms that exist within we human beings during our latter years were not present at the time of our birth. It is therefore incorrect to say that each of us is the sum total of our atoms; we are more than that. It is the configuration of the atoms that counts; the network that links them together.[2] The same is true of our brains: there are some 100 billion neurons in an adult brain; that's fifteen times the number of people on the planet. However, while the quantity of neurons is important, the manner in which they link and interact is crucial. In fact, our brain is a very active network, composed of some 100 trillion connections. If each connection was represented as a star, there would be enough to fill 300 galaxies.[3]

Network theory is crucial in our study of disease. When the human genome project was complete, the hype surrounding it suggested that we were on the brink of curing all known diseases. The US President at that time, Bill Clinton, said in June 2000: "Today, we are learning the language in which God created life. We are gaining ever more awe for the complexity, the beauty, the wonder of God's most divine and sacred gift. With this profound new knowledge, humankind is on the verge of gaining immense, new power to heal. Genome science will have a real impact on all our lives – and even more on the lives of our children. It will revolutionise the diagnosis, prevention and treatment of most, if not all, human diseases." Mr Clinton was not wrong in the general sense. Our growing knowledge of genetic code may indeed provide great insights with extraordinary benefits, but we have learnt that simply mapping it is not enough. The great challenge lies in unravelling the genome network by understanding the links between the nodes. In certain cases, a specific gene has been associated with a specific characteristic; more often it is the interaction of a number of genes that counts. Studying that is far more complex.

It is only when we have built an understanding of the genome network that we will have struck the decisive blow in the war against disease.

---

[2] Steve Grand: *Where do those damn atoms go?*

[3] It is intriguing to think, however, that in the known universe there are roughly a billion times as many stars as there are connections in the brain; were stars interacting in the same way as neurons the resulting processing power would indeed be awesome.

Networks are Emergent

Networks seem to possess a collective consciousness. With one noticeable exception, this appears to be an illusion. Understanding the emergent properties we observe in so many networks is both a fascinating and incredibly important field of study, one which is only just beginning to find traction as an academic discipline.

Slime mould may not be much to behold, but scientists studying emergence seems obsessed with it. For much of their lives the cells that make up slime mould exist as separate single-celled amoeboid protists. Under certain circumstances, usually when conditions are not favourable to survival, they come together to form an ugly swarm, made of these tiny but quite distinct cells. Intriguingly, the swarm seems to portray collective behaviour and can, for example, negotiate its way through a maze using what appears to be memory.[4] What does this mean? Is slime mould a swarm or a single living thing? We can observe tight balls of sardines swimming as if they have a collective intelligence or an ant's nest behaving as if it is a single entity. James Lovelock has even described the Earth as Gaia, a conscious and living organism.[5]

Cities also display emergent properties. If you are a citizen of London you engage in the business of your daily life quite independently of your neighbours. However, if you look at the city as a whole it displays patterns that are not obvious at the individual level. You may, for example, be perfectly relaxed about living next door to someone of a different race or creed. You may not even mind very different people living on either side

---

[4] According to Tetsu Saisuga and his colleagues at Hokkaido University in Sapporo, Japan, you can slow slime mould's movement down by blowing draughts of cold breeze on it. Remove the breeze, and it speeds up. He repeated the experiment three times. Then he stopped the process. But remarkably, the slime mould still moved as if the cold breeze was being blown on it intermittently. So it seems that this swarm of single celled organisms had memory.

[5] Lovelock has christened the Earth Gaia, in part thinking of Isaac Asimov and his Foundation series of books, although Gaia was, according to Greek mythology, the first of the immortals, the grandmother of Zeus. Lovelock is not literally suggesting Gaia is a living organism with a consciousness, although he is not suggesting she isn't that either. But he does say the Earth is an emergent system, which in the case of his theory, may well destroy one of its more dangerous nodes, or bacteria, that dwell on her, namely mankind.

of you. However, you might draw the line at being the only person of your particular grouping on your street. This may seem like a trivial requirement, but studies have shown that while as individuals we may only have a very mild preference for living with like-minded people, when this preference is applied across the city, racial or other groupings soon develop.[6] Likewise, a city can develop into business clusters, with specialists working in a given area. So strong is the pull of these clusters, that they can stay constant for centuries.[7]

Some networks, particularly those found in neurology, collectively form the basis for consciousness. However, I suspect that most do not. Slime mould, ants' nests, cities, the economy, society, the network of computers running the Internet and the World Wide Web may fool us into thinking otherwise, but there are explanations other than consciousness for their behaviour.

Networks are Chaotic Locally yet Organised Systemically

Networks are controlled by the actions of individual agents at the node level oblivious of their effect at the network level. In some cases, nodes behave by copying one another. In others, as seen in animal nervous systems, this occurs through chemical signals. An economist might say it is the transfer of money between nodes which charges the economic network.

Networks appear planned. However, if you zoom in on a network and observe the individual nodes that make it up, they are ignorant of their role in the piece.

---

[6] Thomas Schelling, "Models of segregation"

[7] Steven Johnson says, in *Emergence*: "Imagine a contemporary citizen of Florence who time-travels back eight hundred years, to the golden age of the guilds." He went on to talk about how different the city would be, how lost the modern-day citizen of the city would feel. "And yet," he says, "despite that abject confusion, one extraordinary thing remains constant: our time traveller would still know where to buy a yard of silk. Fast forward a few hundred years, and he'd know where to pick up a gold bracelet, as well. And where to buy leather, gloves, or borrow money. He wouldn't be equipped to buy any of these things, or even to communicate intelligibly to the salesmen – but he'd know where to find the good all the same."

Group order is created from local chaos. Given that, what ties each individual node together? In the case of water, it's hydrogen bonding. In the case of neurons, it's the chemical signal passed from one axon to another. In the case of slime mould, starvation can cause a few of the amoeboid protists to emit pulses called cAMP; others receive the signal, causing them to swarm.

Ants seem to be very organised. If you observe a nest and its legions of ants in action, it is easy to assume that they operate under a command and control hierarchy. If a food source appears within roaming distance of the nest, long lines of ants are soon scurrying between the nest and the food. Looking at such behaviour at face value, one might assume that the ants' nest must be subject to a management structure of some form. The metaphor of the "queen" adds to the illusion. We are fooled into thinking that there's a single leader, reigning supreme, with control over the army at her disposal. She's something of a cross between Margaret Thatcher and Grace Jones, issuing edicts to sergeants, who bark her orders at rank and file soldiers and workers. Hollywood exaggerated that myth as only it can and gave us the film *Ants*. Woody Allen as a worker ant, Sylvester Stallone as a soldier: anthropomorphosis at its finest.

In fact, no such ordered structure exists. Ants interact with each other via chemical compounds called pheromones. Studies appear to show that there are just ten signals that allow ants to communicate with each other, providing such messages as "I am foraging," "there's food over there" and "run away." [8] Furthermore, they change their behaviour depending on the volume of messages being issued. During the course of an hour, if an ant perceives ten others foraging, it responds one way. If it perceives more than 100, its reaction is different. Steven Johnson, in his book *Emergence*, puts it this way: "The colonies take a problem that human societies might solve with a command system (some kind of broadcast from mission control announcing there are too many foragers) and instead solve it using statistical probabilities."

In other words, by following simple rules at the node level, each ant contributes to an extremely "well managed" system. However, the order at the network level emerges from the chaotic behaviour of the ants themselves.

For the economy, an equally simple system creates order: "the price mechanism". If the price is high relative to the cost of production, producers will take on more staff (or get existing workers to work harder) and output will rise. If the price is low, redundancies follow and output declines. Economic theory suggests displaced workers will then be employed elsewhere, perhaps working for a lower wage, producing a different product. Classical economics gives us the laws of supply and demand, and of profit maximisation. Central control is seen as inefficient and unresponsive: the Soviet Union failed partly because its economic system was unworkable. Some producers manufactured too much of a certain good, creating huge and wasteful surpluses; others, following government instructions, produced too little creating unnecessary shortages.[9]

Capitalism appears to be more successful: chaotic nodes (that's you and me) creating "efficient markets". There are other explanations for creating economic order from chaos, however (see chapter 2).

Networks have Structure

The way in which the individual units that constitute a network link with each other is crucial, be they sardines, neurons, people or planets. The degree of separation between nodes determines how effectively a network operates.

In networks, all nodes are connected; a node can be reached from a given start point by following those connections. Studies into network theory have focused on a particular, effective structure called the "small world" model: a good example of this is the network of neurons in your brain. Human society is structured in a similar way.

---

[8] E.O. Wilson and Bert Holldobler – *The Ants*, also see Steven Johnson, *Emergence*, page 75.

[9] Years before the collapse of the Soviet Union, Andrei Amalrik penned the book *Will the Soviet Union survive until 1984?* Amalrik forecast the collapse of the Soviet Empire, precisely because of what he saw as the inefficiencies of the command system. But when the book was published, his hypothesis was ridiculed. Of course, there are many theories as to why the Soviet Union collapsed, among them, that Reagan Star Wars project, which some say was little more than a bluff, forced the Soviet into spending on defence they could not afford – but then again, if the Soviet Economy had been more efficient, maybe it could have more easily kept pace with US defence spending.

Perhaps, whilst on holiday, you've met someone for the first time who knows one of your friends. "It's a small world," you find yourself saying. Stanley Milgram put this idea to the test. Imagine you have in your possession a letter for a certain individual. You know this person's name, occupation, and the region where they live, but you don't know his address. Your task, in Milgram's experiment, is to forward a letter either directly to the target recipient or someone believed to be closer to the person in question.

Milgram wanted to see how many times the letter had to be forwarded on until it reached the intended target. In this experiment every occasion the letter was sent was described as a degree of separation. If, by pure chance, you happened to know the intended person's address and sent the letter directly to them, one degree of separation would exist. Milgram conducted several tests. In one experiment, 296 letters were sent; most went missing. 64 found their target: of those, the chain between the first person and ultimate recipient was, on average, 5.5.

From this experiment came the saying "six degrees of separation".[10]

There is a slight catch with Milgram's original experiment. If you were sent a letter out of the blue and were asked to redirect it as part of an experiment, what would you do? Chances are you would bin it. As such, Milgram's experiment has survivor bias built into it. Chains with more than seven links are likely to have broken down. Subsequent analysis of the Milgram data has suggested that there is an average of 11 links tying people together.[11]

Another famous example of a small world experiment was the so-called "Six Degrees of Kevin Bacon", which was referred to by both Mark Newman in his book *Networks and Introduction* and Albert-László Barabási in *Linked*. Author Richard Gilliam designed a game in which the players had to find how many films linked a randomly selected actor to Kevin Bacon, having appeared in the same film. For example, Elvis Presley appeared in *Change of Habit*, which also starred Edward Asner, who appeared in *JFK* as did Bacon. Elvis is separated from Bacon by two steps: in the jargon of the game, he had a Bacon number of two.

---

[10] See *Psychology Today* 1967, (61-67) "The Small-world-problem" by Stanley Milgram.

[11] Albert, Jeong, and Barabasi 1999.

Incidentally, Kevin Bacon is not particularly "well connected"; Rod Steiger was better connected at the time Gilliam designed his game. Of importance here is the fact that all nodes (actors) in the network (Hollywood) are connected; their degree of connectedness varies and is important in its own right.

Networks are Far Reaching

Relative to the size of the network, individual connections can sometimes stretch a very long way. In the brain, for example, the ability of neurons to interact with others far away is associated with intelligence. Although most networks lack any form of self-awareness, it is worth noting that those associated with consciousness in living creatures have long-reaching connections.

The connections between certain nodes can reach all the way across the network: this is highly significant. In a healthy brain, for example, neurons don't only link to their neighbours, but to others far, far away, on the other side of the cortex. A reduced number of long-distance connections have been observed in temporal lobe dementia, a form of mental illness. Alzheimer's disease has been observed in brains with a higher degree of randomness in neural connectivity.

Recent evidence suggests that consciousness may be associated with the neurons that link between sections of the brain. For example, we may become conscious of information generated in the visual cortex only if those signals are broadcast to many different areas at once.[12]

Research has shown that neurons occasionally work together in a form of perfect harmony, where clusters of neurons fire synchronically. This is called "phase-locking", an expression one might more readily associate with Star Trek. On other occasions neurons fire chaotically. Imagine an orchestra playing a few bars of a melody in unison, followed by a few bars where each musician plays a different tune in a discordant key, each in their own time signature: it would sound like a switch from Mozart to Miles Davis.

---

[12] David Robson, "Disorderly genius: How chaos drives the brain", *New Scientist* 27 June 2009

Such research has demonstrated these fluctuations to be vital. Experiments that compare neural activity to IQ in children have shown that those with longer periods of chaotic firing score more highly; should these periods be longer still, there is a correlation with conditions such as autism."They say it's a fine line between genius and madness," says neuroscientist David Liley from the Swinburne University of Technology in Melbourne, Australia and quoted in New Scientist, "Maybe we're finally beginning to understand the wisdom of this."

Networks Have Hubs

It has been observed time and time again in physics, biology, economics, sociology and anthropology that a small number of the nodes within a network often form hubs, each of which possess more links than the rest. Some of these hubs have a substantially higher number of connections than their counterparts. The distribution of the connectivity of nodes in such networks commonly follows what's called a "power law", with a small number of super-hubs, a larger number of more modestly connected hubs, and the rest; nodes possessing just a few connections.

If you are an actor one link away from Rod Steiger, you are connected by just one additional link to everyone in Steiger's network. Steiger is what network theory would call a hub: he is very well connected, possessing what is known as a high degree of "centrality". Here are two other examples of hubs in networks.

Just over 2000 years ago, a poor carpenter died in an obscure backwater of the Roman Empire. Most of his followers were Jewish, persecuted by their Roman rulers, and few in number. Their creed was unpopular with non-Jews, for several reasons: the fact that to join their religion men had to be circumcised was significant. A wealthy Roman citizen called Saul was converted to the cause. He changed his name to Paul, modified the way this new religion was practised, removed the need for circumcision, and merged into it ideas from the Greco-Roman world. Using his extraordinary network of contacts, he preached his newfound religion in terms his fellow educated Romans and Greeks could understand. Paul was a hub: a highly connected node in the network that was the Roman world.

Gaëtan Dugas was a good-looking Canadian flight attendant. His job entailed him travelling large distances. He was also extremely sexually active within the gay community, claiming to have had over 2500 sexual partners. Unfortunately, he also contracted AIDS. Before dying of kidney failure in 1984, Dugas is thought to have spread AIDS to many hundreds of people and is described as being "patient zero", a central hub in the early spread of the disease in North America. Had Dugas not contracted the illness its spread might have been far slower, giving scientists more time to study it and giving the message of safe sex more time to become widespread. On the other hand, it was inevitable that a hub such as Dugas would be among the first to catch the disease. It is likely that there were not many degrees of separation between the hubs in the network of AIDS sufferers and more peripheral figures that may have contracted the disease earlier.

According to studies by Albert-László Barabási and colleagues at the University of Notre Dame, hubs appear with remarkable constancy in networks ranging from the spread of diseases, the make-up of ecosystems, cells within animals and plants, the economy, and across the Internet, both at the router level or in the Web. For example, in the context of the Web, Google is an exceptionally large hub. It is these hubs that support small world networks: it's a small world because hubs reduce the number of links between one node and another.

Barabási also found that the occurrence of these hubs tends to follow a power law: of a large number of nodes, there are only a small number of hubs, and a smaller number still of "super-hubs".[13]

---

[13] If you were to plot the number of links relating to nodes along a graph with logarithmic scale, then the occurrence of hubs of varying degrees of connectivity would approximately follow a smooth trajectory. These networks, made up of hubs following a power law are known as scale-free. A random network is one in which the number of links pertaining to each vertices is random, and as such the distribution function describing these links follows a normal probability or Gaussian curve, with most vertices having just one or two links, and very few with more than say half a dozen and none with more than say 100. To give an example of a Gaussian network it could describe the spread of heights among, say, adult males. Most will be between five and six feet, a very small number over seven feet and a similar small number under four feet. No one, however, would be 100 feet tall. A scale-free model may be more analogous to one describing wealth. Most people may be worth, say, fifty thousand pounds. But then someone like Warren Buffett may be worth approaching a million times more than that.

Facebook is an excellent example. Within the Facebook network, a large number of us possess 100 or so "friends". Within that number, there is probably one linked to several thousand. Furthermore, certain "super-hubs" within Facebook may have tens of thousands, even hundreds of thousands of connections. Barabási suggests that a number of factors need to be in place for such hubs to emerge. One of these factors is growth. In a growing network, one would expect nodes that have been in existence for longer to have more links.

Such networks are described as being "scale-free".

Another important factor is what is known as preferential attachment. We all intuitively understand the principle of preferential attachment. Imagine two similar cafés opposite each other on the street. The first customer of the day has no preference; he randomly chooses one. The second customer may also be unsure, but is more likely to opt for the café which isn't empty. So, each new customer chooses the same café, until eventually one of the establishments is heaving with customers, the other deserted. This is described as "the rich get richer". Popular nodes may attract links, their very popularity giving them their appeal.

Networks Have Integrity

It appears that scale-free networks are extremely robust. The Internet, for example, is an archetypal example of a scale-free network. With a relatively small number of super-hubs, it is considered to be impervious to most forms of attack. Likewise, Al-Qaeda remains relatively intact after the death of Osama bin Laden. A scale-free network is vulnerable, however, to a focused and simultaneous attack on all its major hubs. These hubs are often the agents of change within the network. However, under certain circumstances, the network can be resistant to change. I suggest that even super-hubs have a relatively trivial influence upon us and that the relationship between the hubs and nodes in the human network suggests that a higher number of poorly connected nodes are far more important than we give them credit for.

Scale-free networks can be remarkably robust: the loss of nodes is not particularly important.

For example, the Internet could lose most of the nodes that make it up, without losing overall cohesion.[14] The robustness of scale-free networks may explain why natural selection has so frequently favoured this form of network. A reason why the global ecosystem survived the catastrophe of the meteorite which wiped out the dinosaurs is that global life network is scale-free. However, scale-free networks are vulnerable to attacks on the hubs, particularly if those attacks cause a cascade. It has been argued that banks are the hubs of the economy. When Lehman Brothers went bust in September 2008, the global financial system lost a super-hub, the shock which cascaded throughout the system, causing the financial crisis. For that reason, it is argued that banks need to be protected to prevent the integrity of the economic network from collapsing. If a bank's behaviour is undesirable, the implications of that argument can be severe indeed given the importance of hubs to the network.

Hubs can be the agents of change within a network. Marketing professionals focus on hubs when launching a new product. In the war against an infectious disease, the most cost-effective solution is to focus on inoculating hubs; this is true, yet controversial. How would society react if we focused on inoculating younger people who travel widely against a disease over older people who may suffer more severe symptoms?

---

[14] In fact the Internet was designed initially by United States Defence Advanced Research Project Agency (ARPA) as a network of computers that could survive a Soviet attack.

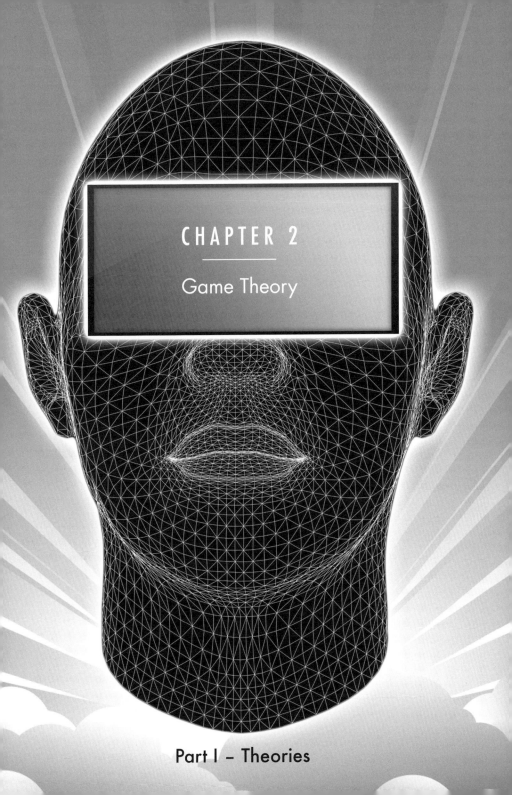

CHAPTER 2

Game Theory

Part I – Theories

CHAPTER 2

Game Theory

Nice, say the iconoclasts, is a word that is too "nice". It's like beige, a word that shows a lack of imagination. Don't say "It's a nice day," say "It's a glorious day". Yet it is hard to think of a word that better describes one of the key characteristics that makes us who we are, for it seems natural selection has favoured a configuration of genes, a network if you like, that makes most of us naturally nice. We do behave selflessly. We do act out of kindness. Our evolution has made us that way. This natural niceness tendency can be explained by a branch of study which fascinates economists and mathematicians alike: game theory. In the jargon of game theory, we don't call it nice. We refer to it as tit-for-tat, or even tit-for-two-tats. This trait is important. Very important. For without it, the human network is unlikely to have developed. As a response system, it may even have been essential for promoting survival across the animal kingdom.

The classic example of game theory is described as the Prisoners' Dilemma: a scenario in which you and one other are being questioned by police for a crime you both committed. The police can prove you committed a less serious crime, but need a confession from either you or your accomplice to prosecute the more serious transgression. The police offer you a deal: freedom if you confess and give the police enough evidence to put the other suspect away. In the event the other suspect confesses too, both of you will be imprisoned for five years. If on the other hand, you keep quiet, and your partner confesses, you are imprisoned for ten years. Finally, if both you and your partner keep quiet, you are both imprisoned for the minor crime, and go inside for six months.

You have no way of communicating with your fellow inmate. What do you do?

Here is another more romantic example of game theory, this time dreamt up by Martin Hollis.[15] This scenario involves two friends, called Adam and Eve,

---

[15] *Reason in Action, essays in the Philosophy of Social Science*, Cambridge University Press, 26 January 1996

who embark on a walk searching for a public house. Along the route they have chosen there are six such establishments, called, in the order that they are passed, The Rational Choice, The Social Contract, The Foole, The Sensible Knave, The Extra Trick and The Triumph of Reason. Adam and Eve have different preferences, but they broadly agree on the pubs they like and dislike. So, one would expect them to stop their walk at a location they both like, although in doing so they may have to compromise by choosing a pub which one may like less than the other.

This table shows the six pubs and their order of preference for each person; the lower the value, the more popular the venue. There are a few simple rules. Adam and Eve can't do a deal. They can only stop at one pub. Whenever they come to a location where one of them wants to stop, they must both stop. After leaving, they must return home.

Order of pubs along the walk	Order of preference for Adam	Order of preference for Eve
The Rational Choice	5	6
The Social Contract	6	4
The Foole	3	5
The Sensible Knave	4	2
The Extra Trick	1	3
The Triumph of Reason	2	1

Where should they stop? The Triumph of Reason would surely be the best choice; it's Adam's second favourite and Eve's favourite. Unfortunately game theory would suggest they would end up at the first, a ghastly establishment.

This is why. Adam prefers The Extra Trick to The Triumph of Reason, so would want to stop before reaching the end of the walk. Eve prefers The Sensible Knave to The Extra Trick. She's aware that Adam will want to stop at his favourite pub, so will decide to stop at The Sensible Knave. Adam will second guess this and will therefore choose The Foole. Eve dislikes the Foole, so instead will choose The Social Contract. Since this is Adam's least favourite pub he will choose The Rational Choice. In other words, a rational decision-making process would mean the two of them would end up stopping at a pub they both dislike, irrespective of the fact that one of them dislikes it more than the other.

The mathematician Charles Nash (the subject of the film *A Beautiful Mind* starring Russell Crowe) devised a method for calculating this rational choice in game theory, a choice which has been called the Nash Equilibrium. For Adam and Eve, the Nash Equilibrium would be the Rational Choice. In the Prisoners' Dilemma, the Nash Equilibrium would involve both you and your fellow criminal confessing, landing you both with a five year prison sentence, and not the six months you'd have gone down for had you both stayed quiet. A society or an economy in which the Nash Equilibrium always applies would be a very unpleasant place to live. Rarely would we enjoy optimal satisfaction.

For creating order from chaos across the economy, the price mechanism has a rival: tit-for-tat. The political scientist Robert Axelrod subjected prisoners' dilemma type situations to various tests. He found that the technique that seemed to be most effective at creating the best possible outcome was one he called "tit-for-tat". In this model, he assumed that the scenario is ongoing and that each player, be they Adam or Eve or one of the two prisoners, play multiple rounds swapping roles from one round to the next.

In the tit-for-tat scenario, each participant in the test initially works on the assumption that other players will be more thoughtful and selfless in their choice. So, in the case of Adam and Eve's walk, Eve assumes Adam will choose The Triumph of Reason. She will then respond the next time the game is played by making a similarly selfless decision. But, in the tit-for-tat situation, if one of the agents involved defects and plays unfair by maximising their enjoyment at the expense of other players, in the next round this player will be punished. So, if Adam chooses to stop at The Extra Trick, during the following round Eve will choose The Sensible Knave.

In other words, each player behaves in a way that is in the best interest of everyone: if one player defects, there is a "tit" response for the original "tat".

Tit-for-tat appears to explain many of our observations of nature, society and the economy. However, in the real world a degree of subtlety is added in that tit-for-tat may operate on a one-degree-removed basis. To explain, consider a networking group. A member of this group can expect occasional assistance from other members, but in return is expected to provide help back to other members. They are not necessarily expected to offer help to the same member who provided the initial help. So it may work as follows: person A provides a favour to person B, who provides a favour to person C, who provides a favour to person A.

Axelrod took tit-for-tat one step further: tit-for-two-tats, where an agent must default twice before being punished. This can be an important strategy. It is not hard to see how a tit-for-tat strategy can lead to hatred. Consider the Montagues and the Capulets. Shakespeare did not clarify how the feud between the two families began. But, what is clear is that the situation had worsened over time. So, Tybalt threatens Romeo with death, Mercutio fights Tybalt but is killed, Romeo avenges his friend's death by killing Tybalt.

Vendettas are the stuff of history. Tit-for-tat killings can go on for generations. Such was surely a major part of the troubles in Northern Ireland, until a few years ago. But how can we end such a feud? Mercutio's solution was for a "plague on both your houses". Perhaps of greater benefit would be to give transgressors a second chance. Could a tit-for-two-tats strategy stop feuds in their tracks?

To put tit-for-tat into the language of the network, individual nodes may interact with others in an apparently selfless way: such behaviour, when extrapolated across the network, creates an environment of cooperation. Robin Dunbar in his book *How Many Friends Does One Person Need?: Dunbar's Number and Other Evolutionary Quirks* has suggested that in the days when we were hunter-gatherers we lived in communities of around 150. In such a tight community of *Homo sapiens sapiens*, it is not hard to see how tit-for-tat would have worked, and how the community would have reacted to an individual acting in their own self-interest.

We may no longer live in isolated pockets of 150 people; we live in cities, have hundreds of friends on our Facebook or LinkedIn accounts and interact with thousands of people over the course of our lifetime. However, tit-for-tat defines the way in which we interact with others. Our evolution may have hardwired into us a tendency to follow tit-for-tat; society may have moulded us. Either way, it seems that such a response system is the means by which the nodes in the human network interact with each other, far more so than naked self-interest or money.

Crucially, it is a key factor in the creation and maintenance of the collaboration and cooperation required for innovation. Without such a response system, in a society governed by the Nash Equilibrium, we might still be living in caves.

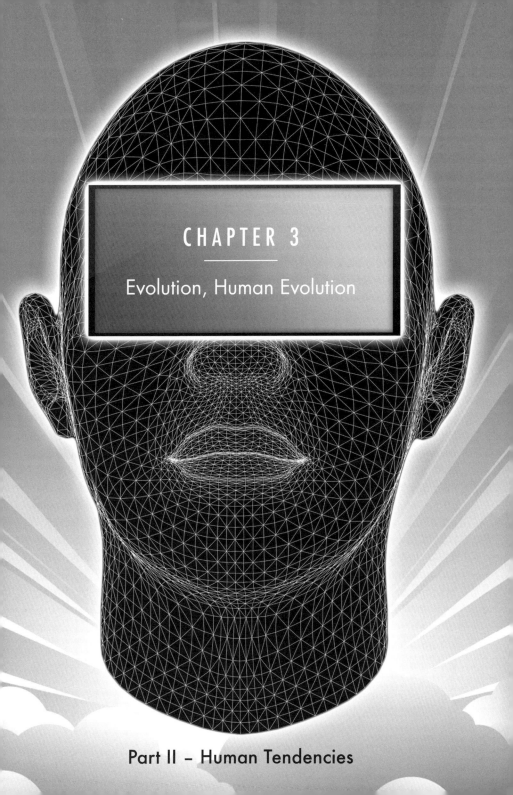

CHAPTER 3

Evolution, Human Evolution

Part II – Human Tendencies

CHAPTER 3

Evolution, Human Evolution

When Dean Friedman and Denise Marsa once sang: "You can thank your lucky stars that we're not as smart as we'd like to think we are," it is possible they were on to something. They continued: "We can thank our lucky stars that we're not as smart as we'd like to think we are". It's the last few words of that song I find to be particularly poignant. If Friedman, who was the songwriter behind that piece, had managed to wrap a few psychological studies around that statement, had done some research of his own and been able to draw scientific evidence to back up his core hypothesis, I reckon he would have been in the running for a Nobel Prize.

The truth is that we are not.

Not Evolved Enough

Consider the theory put forward by the anthropologist Robin Dunbar. The professor found a correlation between the skull size of certain primates and the typical size of the community they lived in. Gibbons, for example, which boast quite small crania, live in communities of five to six. The bigger-brained chimps typically mix in communities of between 50 and 80. Extrapolating the trajectory Dunbar believed he had identified, he concluded that the cognitive limit to the number of people we can hold stable relationships with is 148. This number has been rounded up such that the Dunbar Number is said to be 150. Contemporary hunter-gatherers live in groups of around 150. Early Neolithic villages, the remains of which have been found in Mesopotamia, had accommodation for approximately 150. The smallest unit of independent troops in the army is close to this number: 135 in the British Army and 200 in the US Army. This begs the question "Why?" Dunbar reckons it all boils down to social bonding. Chimps promote social cohesion via grooming. For humans, living in larger communities, grooming is not practical. Instead we need language, a superior communication tool.

The challenge today is that we live and interact in networks made up of far more than 150 human nodes. We had evolved abilities and skill sets that were perfect for the first 95% of our existence as a species living among 150 or so others. Those characteristics seem less than ideal today.

A literal translation of *Homo sapiens* is "wise man", but are we wise men of technology or of the modern economy? While living a life of hunting and gathering we were indeed wise men – the wise men of the plains. For most of our 150,000 to 200,000 years we have been hunter-gatherers, our lives were relatively simple. It also appears we were relatively healthy too. Arthritis, repetitive strain injury, rotten teeth, osteoarthritis and dreadful diseases such as tuberculosis, leprosy, cholera and malaria were either first experienced or became a lot more common after the establishment of agriculture and the switch to living in large communities. As Christopher Stringer and Robin McKie say in their book, *African Exodus*, "… agriculture had a devastating effect on health".

A city lifestyle and a diet based on agriculture do not seem to be well supported by our evolutionary history. One might be forgiven for being filled with longing for those simpler times although, no doubt, we look back with rose-tinted spectacles. However, it is clear that the complex world we live in today is challenging for us. As soon as we began farming, *Homo sapiens* had bitten into the apple that permanently exiled us from the Garden of Eden.[16] It's not all bad news: we are highly adaptable; our cause is not hopeless. Nonetheless, there are very real problems with us as an evolved species, which we simply must fix using that wisdom of ours.

When Did It Stop?

What Charles Darwin referred to as evolution is not an automatic process. Change and adaptation is not something that occurs by default. Rather, it needs a catalyst, a reason for nature to favour a new mutation. Even then, change is not guaranteed.

Consider the Theory of Punctuated Equilibrium, as postulated by Stephen J. Gould and Niles Eldredge. They propose that in large populations, mutations that confer certain advantages tend to get diluted: that the large

---

[16] You may of course ask, if agriculture is so bad why did it take hold? Jared Diamond, in his book *Guns, Germs and Steel*, Vintage Books, 1997, argued that what agriculture did achieve was to allow populations to grow bigger, and that these superior numbers gave agricultural societies military advantage over hunter-gatherers; as a result agricultural societies began to spread via conquest.

populations have a homogenising effect. Gould and Eldredge argue that for the evolutionary process to produce a successful mutation, a much smaller subgroup of the species must first become isolated. In this way, the mutation can take hold and become dominant within this subset. Later, when this isolated subgroup is reunited with the main population the mutation is sufficiently developed for it to become widespread. The subset where such a change took control would be so small that it is unlikely that evidence of the original mutation could be found in the fossil record; consequently we see the change only when that subset is reassumed into general population. The fossil record then provides evidence of sudden and abrupt changes in a species, not a gradual shift.

Another theory, developed by Elisabeth Vrba of Yale University, known as the Turnover Pulse Hypothesis, argues that change is almost entirely absent from the fossil record for long periods of time, and that when it occurs it is correlated with external developments, such as climate change or another environmental factor. What these theories both suggest is that Darwinian evolution is not a slow, bit by bit process: it works in fits, starts and jumps.

Look at it from a network perspective. The network representing a species, or an ecosystem, is highly complex. Change requires a rewiring of the network; there is inbuilt resistance to this. We too easily assume that as our technology and culture advances our physical make-up and DNA adapts to suit. But, as the theories of Punctuated Equilibrium and the Turnover Pulse Hypothesis suggest, such adaptations are unlikely to have occurred.[17]

Are You Good with Numbers?

One way in which our evolution does not favour our modern lifestyle relates to our innate perception of maths and our understanding of probability. Imagine you are on a game show. There are three doors: behind one is a

---

[17] This is not to say our evolution has stopped altogether. One obvious example of how humans who are isolated from each other have evolved is skin colour. Our ability to digest certain foods is another example. Take milk: it appears lactose tolerance is a relatively new adaptation and indeed one that does not apply across humanity. Tolerance for alcohol is a third example. In Europe we mixed alcohol with water in order to purify it; in the East it was more common to boil water and mix it with leaves such as tea. However, none of these observations detract from the point: that the majority of the cognitive abilities that became hardwired into us to facilitate survival during our hunter gatherer past have not mutated to suit a modern world in which we interact within much larger, closely-knit populations.

car; behind the other two a goat. You have two guesses. You choose the first door. The host, who knows where the car is, opens one of the other two doors, revealing a goat. He asks you to guess again. Do you change your mind, or stay put?

Most of us would say it makes no difference: the chances are equal. You would be wrong. In fact, the probability of the car being behind the original door is one in three, but behind the other door, it is one in two. If you are anything like me, you will struggle with that problem. That, in a nutshell, is the difficulty. This problem was in fact originally described by Marilyn vos Savant, in *Parade Magazine* back in 1990. It has been the subject of many studies since. Michael Shermer elegantly summarised the problems in *Scientific American*, October 2008: "We never evolved a probability network and thus folk intuitions are ill equipped to deal with many aspects of the modern world."

During the course of our lives we experience myriad events. Occasionally, as the law of averages dictates, we observe spooky coincidences. Sometimes, we stumble on a brilliant idea; on other occasions we are lucky. There is a danger of viewing these inevitable occurrences through the prism of our perspective, and see a cause or a pattern, which actually does not exist. The law of averages suggests some kids will develop autism soon after having an MMR jab. However, this does not mean the jab caused the condition. The chances of intelligent life appearing on a planet may be one in a million, but for the sentient being of that planet it may seem as if the coincidence of their existence proves a mystical process was at work.

Consider a league made of twenty football teams of varying quality. We all know that in a sporting event the outcome is unpredictable: as illustrated by the fact that underdogs do win. Assume that the best team in the league play the worst team one hundred times, the best team might win fifty matches, the worst team might win twenty, and the rest would be drawn. So, there is a one in five chance the worst team will win. This would also mean there is a one in twenty-five chance the worst team will beat the best team twice in a row. This simple law of statistics suggests that on occasions one of the worst five teams in this league will beat all of the top five teams twice during the course of the season. It is also quite possible that occasionally one of the worst teams will win the league. And yet we watch and say, of our team, "... they are a strange bunch. When we play against the very best opponent, our players excel themselves; for the rest of the season we play badly." Or, we may question events: "Why is it that our team won the league last year, but is in danger of relegation this year?" We look for an explanation and conclude that good opposition brings the best out of our players; that they have lost confidence; or that the manager has lost his touch.

It would be equally true to claim that there is no reason, and that randomness is to blame. Leonard Mlodinow of the California Institute of Technology, used the metaphor "The Drunkard's Walk" in his book of that name to explain the idea. Nassim Taleb explored a similar idea in his book *Fooled by Randomness*. It is possible that randomness plays a much larger role in life than we realise.

I can feel very sorry for the managers of football teams: they get fired if their team suffers a run of bad results. You wouldn't fire someone if they call the toss of a coin wrong five times in a row. However, the dismissal of coaches can be analogous to that. On the other hand, coaches are not shy in coming forward when their team does well. They get paid handsomely for it. It is not dissimilar to the behaviour of central bankers: taking credit when things go well, deferring blame when they go badly.

A banker is someone who draws rich plaudits when the forces of randomness smile. However, when things turn bad merely forgoes a bonus; or at worse, perhaps loses a job. Providing sufficient money is made during the good times, the loss of a job may be a price well worth paying. Likewise, a fund may outperform all others in its sector five years in a row. Is that because the fund manager is brilliant? Perhaps, but randomness might have produced the same results.

As Taleb said, we are often fooled by randomness, preferring to select an individual upon whom to heap praise.

The phrase "regression to the mean" is relevant here. If an investment delivers a one-hundred-fold return, we can be fooled into thinking we had more influence than actually we did. Should we repeat our efforts many times, regression to the mean may mean our average performance is more mediocre. A sportsman, or pop star, or serial entrepreneur, may enjoy a run of success, but the more often they try to repeat their success, the more likely regression to the mean will occur.

Mlodinow tells the story of Sherry Lansing, top brass at Paramount, who commissioned *Forrest Gump*, *Braveheart* and *Titanic*. She was a "genius", who then "lost her touch". She was fired, following one flop after another. In the year or so after her departure, the studio enjoyed a run of hits. So, its decision to fire Lansing was proven right, or so it appeared. However, films such as *War of the Worlds* and *The Longest Yard* had already begun under Lansing's tenure. Mlodinow also quotes a Hollywood executive who reportedly said: "If I had said yes to all the projects I turned down, and no to all the other ones I took, it would have worked out about the same."

We can be fooled into finding reason and explanation in results that are down to sheer randomness. Does it matter? One side effect of this behaviour is the tendency to find patterns in chaos which means that we see examples of the existence of a misidentified pattern; we ignore any evidence to the contrary. From those tendencies, we become superstitious; we look for truth in astrology and can place our faith in certain beliefs. I return to this later on.

We're a Risky Bunch

Our evolution has reinforced characteristics relating to extreme risk-taking and arrogance. As we shall see later, this is not all bad. Nonetheless, it can explain some of our more unpleasant characteristics.

This one confused even Darwin. How do you explain suicidal bees? They will attack a threat to their hive, even though in so doing they sign their own death warrants? Or what about the ants, serving the queen and her young, living without the chance to reproduce themselves? How can evolution throw up such behaviour? It boils down to what's called "inclusive fitness". Evolution throws up traits if those traits can help propagate the genes of a creature that practises them. If an animal sacrifices its life but in the process saves the lives of its offspring, then it is advancing the course of its DNA. So an ant, for example, whose DNA is shared by other members of the nest, has a reason to help promote the success of that nest. That's one of the big advantages of big families. In the ants' nest, beehive, or wasp nest, families are pretty big; there is just the one mother and father for the entire community. So, from the point of view of Darwinian evolution, suicidal behaviour is quite rational, so long as some of your own DNA is passed into the next generation.

Equally, belligerence, bravery and extreme risk taking may serve a purpose.

Take as an example a Mongolian tribal chief called Tamujin. He was a risk taker, growing up in a country of extreme violence. Many of his countrymen suffered bloody deaths. While still very young, Tamujin himself, killed his own half brother. Yet, from the point of view of Tamujin's DNA it appears this high risk strategy paid off. So numerous were the children he fathered that he spread his family's DNA far and wide. Today, no less than 16 million men can claim descent from that warrior. For Tamujin was also known as the universal ruler, the great king, Genghis Khan.

Scientists Laurent Lehmann and Marc Feldman reckon they have been able to show how there is a good reason why behavioural traits such as belligerence and bravery may have evolved. This is not to say that a risk taker sees their strategy in terms of propagating their DNA. Darwinian evolution does not work like that. It confers traits on us, without feeling the need to explain them. A man who sees a girl he fancies does not immediately think "Cor blimey. Think of the healthy children she'll raise." The parts of the female he may find attractive may well provide those benefits; his own thoughts are likely to be somewhat less profound. Likewise, a young foolhardy male does not think: "My behaviour makes sense. If my brothers and I behave like this, at least one of us will be highly successful at mating. Let's attack the tribe next door, and steal all of their women. Only one of us has to breed."

On the contrary, the foolhardy male, the warrior with battle-lust truly believes he will be the successful one. His expectations may not be realistic, but his poor sense of risk assessment serves a purpose. Maybe it is this same trait that encourages the risks taken by gamblers, by entrepreneurs, by adrenalin junkies. Risk takers have confidence in their ability, in the inevitability of their success. While they are blind to reality, blind to the harm they may cause themselves, in terms of propagating DNA it serves a purpose.

Perhaps the thrusting masculinity seen amongst bankers during that period before the financial crisis, often blamed as the main cause of the disaster, may have been a simple case of genes put there by Darwinian evolution exerting themselves.

It Pays to be Nice

Even though we possess natural abilities and traits evolved for our role as hunter-gatherers, it does not mean these characteristics are either an irrelevance or a nuisance today. In fact, some have come in rather handy; we have skills and traits that are far more useful than we realise. We may not be as smart as we think we are, but we're a good deal nicer.

The evolution of an "altruistic gene" serves a purpose. If you are sitting on a train opposite someone with a nasty cold, it may serve your interest to offer them a tissue. Likewise, it can make sense for a pigeon that spots a hawk high in the sky to alert fellow pigeons; if the flock were to immediately rush for cover, the chaos might distract the hawk for a sufficiently long period of time to save everyone. If, on the other hand, the pigeon moved only to save itself, its behaviour may have singled it out to the hawk: this is a big risk. In other words, behaviour that may seem unselfish serves a purpose, supporting the evolution of the genes lending themselves to altruistic behaviour.

Vampires, as we know them, are bloodthirsty creatures that enjoy the discomfort and fear of their prey. Can even vampires display altruistic behaviour? Unfortunately, vampires have been less than forthcoming to scientists seeking volunteers; the cast of *Twilight* were busy that day. However, the good news is that they were able to study vampire bats. What is quite extraordinary about these creatures is that they can be surprisingly unselfish. For it appears a hungry vampire bat will be willing to vomit up its lunch in order to provide nutrition to one of its group that is starving. Quite extraordinary behaviour, when you think about it. It's like a thirsty man giving up a glass of water for someone else who is suffering from greater thirst.

Why would bats evolve such behaviour? The explanation runs like this:

If all vampire bats are willing to behave altruistically to save their starving fellows, a safety net is created. Any bat in the community who fails to succeed during successive forays will not become increasingly weak; they will not surely die. Those bats who have hunted successfully on a given day might not be so successful during the next. By removing the issue of individual success, through spreading the success (and failure) of the group across all of its members, a form of benefit system exists: contribute when you can, take when you need.[18]

Examine the development of a "niceness" gene from a Darwinian perspective and its purpose is evident. But, it is a purpose we are not necessarily aware of: random chance gave us a "nice" gene and natural selection favoured it. Economic theory may suggest we are naturally selfish: I am delighted to assert that this one core assumption is wrong, and it's wrong for a pretty glorious reason: it's in our genes.

Rewiring Your Brain

We should celebrate the way chance has given us characteristics that prove useful today. However, the respects in which we are limited can be a problem. The question is: How do we change?

Imagine you were raised by wolves. Would you become a Romulus or a Remus? Would you build a great civilisation? Perhaps you might turn out like Mowgli and, having appreciated the bare necessities of life, return to your village to chase girls. Ultimately, it depends on your age at the point of reintegration. There seems to be a point of no return: beyond a certain age, it is unlikely that you would ever be "normal".

It has been suggested that our brains wire themselves during the early, formative years of our lives: once the neural connections have formed, once the hubs and nodes are established, they are difficult to change. This is a widely proposed theory; the argument is as follows: humans are born with a remarkably underdeveloped brain. Were humans born with a fully developed brain, as with other mammals, our heads would have to be substantially larger at birth. On that basis, pregnancies would be longer and childbirth significantly more painful. Without substantial changes to the female anatomy, it is quite possible that delivery would be nearly impossible. Darwinian evolution has favoured this, for obvious reasons. So, during the first months of our lives, our brains complete the process of development; our skulls enlarge and strengthen, the neurons in our brain begin to form connections.

---

[18] *The Selfish Gene*, by Richard Dawkins, Oxford University Press, 1976.

Key stages have been identified in our learning: during the first four years the neural networks required for shape, colour, perspective and balance are formed; the first ten years are vital for learning language through developing fine-control over our mouths and tongues, as well as developing skills related to literacy, numeracy and musicianship.

This is known as the "window of opportunity"; the theory is not proven, nor is it unchallenged.

Other evidence suggests that the networks in our brain are reforming all the time: the brain has "plasticity". This theory is afforded support through the study of stroke victims. Such patients often have to re-learn the skills they had developed during their younger years. And frequently, they succeed. You don't need to read reams of literature to know that changing someone's mind is hard. Be honest: how often do you change your mind? It seems that the older we become, the harder it is to change. Our tendencies to form bias play a large role. Our susceptibility to prejudice and preconception strengthens and reinforces our views, galvanising us against change. The network of neurons, once wired, is resistant to disconnection or reconnection, even if neuroplasticity allows it to do so.

While it is difficult to change the perceptions of an individual, changing the view of a group is more challenging still. The group mind becomes set in stone, irrespective of the individual intelligence of its members. As Professor Scott E. Page, University of Michigan, said: "Groups made up of intelligent people who are inwardly diverse – that is, who have different perspectives, mindsets and ways of solving problems – can make more accurate predictions and solve problems more effectively than groups of "experts".

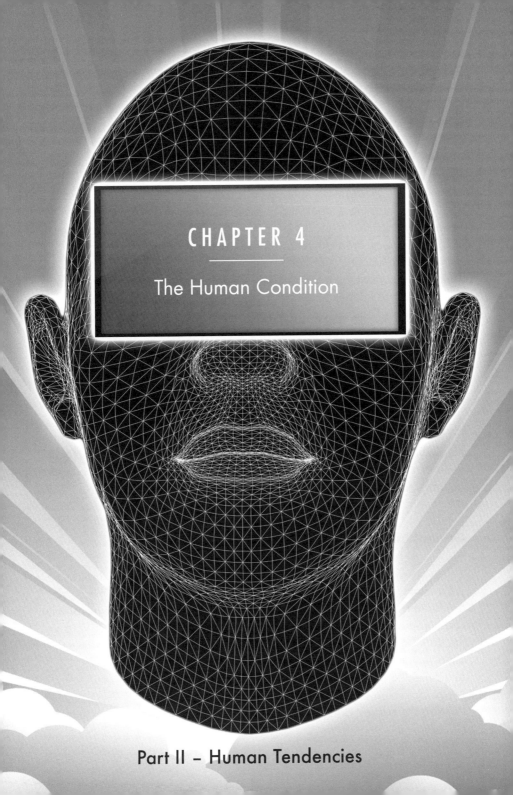

CHAPTER 4

The Human Condition

Part II – Human Tendencies

CHAPTER 4

The Human Condition

"All the world old is queer," said the Welsh industrial philanthropist Robert Owen, "save thee and me, and even thou art a little queer."

That's the interesting thing about us humans: we are complex creatures. To each and every one of us, the behaviour of others can seem odd at times. While we are all prone to certain biases and prejudices, it seems most of us think these limitations are more expressed in those other than ourselves. That's the nature of the human condition. Although we live in groups where our survival may depend on that group, we are inclined to believe that these trappings and failings do not pertain to us. Clearly, they belong to someone else. As soon as we become aware of how biased people can be, we assume that the bias lies with others; the more they disagree with us, the more likely we are to put it down to their prejudice and lack of objectivity. Perversely, a clear understanding of bias can convince us even more of our own rectitude.

"There's now't as queer as folk." These days, economists are waking up to the reality that in order to advance their understating of the economy, they need to grasp what makes folk tick. As far as I'm concerned, it all boils down to how we combine that peculiar sense of confidence we have in with the need to play well in the team.

Groupthink

When crowds come together, groupthink takes root. Sometimes this can yield impressive results; it may have done much to underpin the march of civilisation. On other occasions, groupthink supports extreme views, blindly creating a form of mass socio-economic suicide, as we stumble forward in the dark, following each other to our doom. It is hard to change a group's mind too as the various biases we are all prone to help reinforce our attachment to the group, or network.

Perhaps the biggest danger arising from the weaknesses of our evolution lies in a concept known as "groupthink". Much of the earlier studies into this phenomenon were carried out by the late Yale psychologist Irving Janis.

Groupthink is not necessarily a bad thing; indeed, it can be very important in charging progress. Looking further back, it is not hard to appreciate that during our history as hunter-gatherers, group cohesion was essential. Consider two communities of hunter-gatherers: one made up of free spirits and individual thinkers forever questioning each other, the second group unified by a kind of tacit consent not to go against the grain of the community. Which one would come on top? The archaeologist Professor Clive Gamble, quoted in Christopher Stririger and Robin Mckie's book, *African Exodus*, seems to be in no doubt: "There would have been no room for individual iconoclasts then," he said, "lack of cooperation meant death."

In fact, Jason Shogren, an economist at the University of Wyoming in Laramie, and quoted in *New Scientist* "Free trade may have finished off Neanderthals" by Celeste Biever, says there is even some evidence to suggest that specialisation, which requires interaction within a crowd, is what gave us victory over the Neanderthals.

Consider also those occasions where unity has been crucial. Recall the spirit of the Blitz, and how Britain pulled together during the Second World War. Individual iconoclasts, who held to the doctrine we call pacifism, were much despised by the rest of society. However, without that specific kind of groupthink, Britain may well have lost.

You Aren't Biased?

We are all prone to bias.

Firstly, there's the confirmation bias. We form a certain opinion; once formed we see evidence all around us that proves we are right, by largely ignoring evidence that we are wrong. We all do it subconsciously. Imagine how the confirmation bias, when thrown into a network of individuals possessed of charismatic hubs, can be even more strongly exhibited. This is the stuff that war is made of. With overwhelming evidence to support their respective views, the United States becomes convinced Iran is part of the Axis of Evil; Iran is convinced that the US is the Great Satan.

Then, there's the recency bias. According to Blalock et al, *The Impact of 9/11 on Road Fatalities*, more people died in car accidents as an indirect consequence of the terrorist attacks of 9/11 than occurred on the day itself: people avoided flying and took to a more risky form of transport, the motor car. As another example, sales of lottery tickets from a store where a winning ticket was purchased often rise during the following week. (Guryan and Kearney, *Gambling at Lucky Stores*)

Another example is hindsight bias. When the past is examined with the benefit of hindsight, we often forget our original views and resort to claiming "... of course, I said that all along." Or, there's the Illusion of Small Numbers, which describes how we expect a small sample to conform to the laws of probability. So, we may allow ourselves to be unduly influenced by an insignificant amount of data: should it be unusually cold during a weekend in August, people may assume global warming is a fallacy. Equally, given an unusually warm fortnight in March, we might take that as proof the world is getting hotter. The sweater worn during a particularly good day becomes the "lucky sweater". To cite an extreme example, a few kids in several million develop autism soon after having the MMR vaccination: some conclude the jab caused the autism.

Closely linked with many of these biases is what the philosopher David Hume called the problem of induction. We draw conclusions from empirical evidence but we have no way of knowing whether the evidence was thrown up by the force of randomness, or external circumstances which may not be repeated.

What Holds Us Together?

The network needs glue; in the human network, this comes from the aspects of our psychology that concern spirituality, language and storytelling. Religion may not be the only adhesive that holds a human network together. It is possible that language, our usage of the metaphor and our tradition of storytelling come together to create a trinity of cohesion.

Religion

Whether you are a believer or not, it is clear that religion provides reinforcement to the network of human society. It ties us together creating unity of incredible strength. If you live in a small dormitory town or village, chances are you don't know many of your neighbours. If you, along with every other member of your local community, went to the same building every week to pray, or met up from time to time for religious events, the difference would be considerable. It is easy to imagine that as hunter-gatherers, beliefs in deities helped cement the essential unity of the tribe, creating rituals which in turn help enhance group cohesion.

Religion also imposes rules.

Take, for example, tit-for-tat as an essential mechanism for cooperation. Imagine an experiment involving two subjects. Subject one is given a sum of money, but is required to share some with subject two. Subject two can accept or refuse the offer. In the event that they turn down the offer, the prize is lost: both subjects lose out. In the terminology of game theory, subject two can punish subject one, but in so doing pays a penalty. Before deciding whether to punish or not, subject two is exposed to subliminal messaging, displaying certain words such as holy, pious, divine and religious. After the tests, subjects were asked if they had donated money to a religious organisation over the previous year.

The test, conducted by psychologist Ryan McKay from the Royal Holloway University of London found that those who said they had donated money tended to exact more severe punishments, but only if they had been shown the subliminal messages. Mckay told Andy Coghlan at *New Scientist* magazine "We think that the cues give them a reminder they are being watched. To please the supernatural agent they worship, they exact higher punishments. The other possibility is that the cued words awakened the concepts of appropriate punishment in their minds." He added: "The answer may be that these sacrifices enable the group to secure more cooperation. The punishing may be unpleasant but it's in the service of the greater good for that particular group or religion, enabling them to thrive and spread the word." This experiment shows how religion reinforces tit-for-tat, a key mechanism for facilitating cooperative behaviour.

It is important to understand that evolution is not perfect. It has neither vision nor perspective. It can take a condition or experience that has occurred naturally; if that condition or experience offers benefits, the result is survival. If there are strong disadvantages, the result is extinction. Consequently, in our evolution certain conditions or forms of perception may have been favoured because they helped promote a belief which cemented group cohesion. Our ability to experience "near death experience" (NDE) may fit into this category.

Scientists have been able to cause artificial NDEs to occur using electric currents. Kevin Nelson, a professor of neurology from the University of Kentucky has been studying NDEs, and reckons they are a kind of halfway house between dreaming and consciousness. Quoted in *The Observer*, Nelson told Ian Sample: "These experiences cross cultural boundaries; they are wired deeply within our brain. I think it helps give us a perspective of our place in the universe and by understanding how our brain works during these spiritual experiences, it gives us new insight into who we are." I suspect it may be a similar story with schizophrenia. A side effect of this condition is to hear voices. Google "shaman and schizophrenia" and you will be inundated with links to web sites exploring the idea that the two are in some way connected.

I make no mystic claims here. I am simply suggesting that if religion plays a key, perhaps vital, role in supporting group cohesion, is it not possible evolution may favour a gene that can lead to schizophrenia?

As Michael Moyer says in *Scientific American* August 2009 "Evolutionary Biologists Stephen Jay Gould and Richard Lewontin of Harvard University proposed that religious thinking is a side effect of tendencies that more concretely help humans to thrive." I suspect, however, Gould and Lewontin were understating the truth: religious thinking provides glue for the network. Without it, we may never have evolved away from other earlier versions of hominids.

Words

Take the Sapir-Whorf Hypothesis, first proposed back in the 1920s and 1930s and referred to by Steven Pinker in his book *The Stuff of Thought*. Both Edward Sapir and his student Benjamin Whorf preached the idea of linguistic determinism: that our thoughts are determined by our language. The classic example often cited when mentioning this theory relates to the Inuit people of North America who have a huge number of words for snow. It is argued that as a result they somehow see snow differently, that they do not see snow in its broader sense: they can't, as it were, see the snow for the snow flakes. These days, linguistic determinism, is not widely accepted. Steven Pinker put his criticism well in his book, *The Stuff of Thought*, when he said that the Inuit "... pay more attention to varieties of snow because they have more words for it is so topsy-turvy that it's hard to believe it would be taken seriously were it not for the feeling of cleverness it affords at having transcended common sense".

However, while language may be an important social adhesive, it is an innovation relating to a particular aspect of speech that may prove to be more important. This is a linguistic phenomenon that can both create insights and limitations in groupthink. It is likely to be a cause for innovation, but is also a key source of collective errors as made by human society.

Metaphor

The metaphor is more important than most of us realise. Steven Mithen, speculates in his book, *The Prehistory of the Mind*, that our ability to think and talk in metaphors gave our species, *Homo sapiens sapiens,* a crucial advantage over our cousins *Homo sapiens neanderthalensis.*

To give an example of how our usage of metaphors can help advance understanding, consider the molecular structure of benzene; a problem that preoccupied scientists during the middle years of the 19th century. It took a dream to solve the riddle. Friedrich August Kekule von Stradonitz had been puzzling over the problem, when finally sleep took him. He dreamt of Ouroboros, a circular symbol depicting a serpent eating its own tail. Kekule woke up to a "eureka" moment. He had cracked it. Benzene, he reasoned, was akin to Ouroboros: a ring of carbon atoms. To be frank, the analogy with Ouroboros was not precise, but that doesn't matter.

Metaphors don't need to be exact. Without them, we may well have come unstuck. Richard Dawkins is a great user of the metaphor: "selfish gene" and "blind watchmaker", for example. Or, consider Taleb's "black swan". Taleb uses this metaphor to describe rare and unexpected economic events, such as stock market crashes or banking crises, which when they occur force us to redefine our understanding. The atom, with its nucleus and orbiting electrons is a tiny solar system. We use metaphors taken from current technology to express the workings of the brain and its interaction with the mind.

So, at one stage, the metaphor that was used drew upon clockwork. Then, the brain became analogous to a steam engine. More recently, we use the computer as our metaphor: hardware relating to the brain and software to the mind. Today, we liken the brain and mind to a network like the Internet.

Another good example is the term "evolution". When we use the word evolution, we think of Darwin and his theory of natural selection. So, we may say that a product, or an idea, or a book "evolved". In fact, if we are using the word as a metaphor for Darwin's theory, we are in error. The problem seems not so much our use of the word evolution, but rather with Darwin's. The word was first used by John Lyell: he really did mean it in the literal context of steady progress. It is derived from the Latin, evolvere, meaning "unroll".

Darwin's theory does not describe a steady flow of progress. His theory does not suggest that each step in the evolutionary process is necessarily better than the previous. Darwinian evolution works by trial and error, failure being a far more common occurrence than success. Indeed, Darwin himself did not even use the word evolution until the 6th edition of his famous *Origin of Species* work. Evolution, as envisaged by Darwin, throws up as many solutions as possible in given circumstances: the solutions that work least effectively die out. If circumstances change, it is possible an older adaptation, extinct and never to return, may actually have provided a superior solution to solving the new set of problems than those that had since emerged.

As a result, there is often a common misunderstanding of how evolution works. My son is taller than me, I am taller than my father when he was still alive, and he towered over my grandfather. That's evolution, people say. It's not, at least not in the Darwinian sense. Each generation is taller than the previous one largely because of a superior diet. Rewind the clock back to an era before the invention of agriculture, and we were just as big as the youngest generation today.

So, we use the word evolution as a metaphor and in doing so, we misunderstand Darwin. Ironically, we are using the word correctly in its literal sense. In fact, it was Darwin who was mistaken. We, in turn, build upon that mistake, misunderstand his theory, and compound our error through the metaphor. This reinforces our misunderstanding. And yet, there is a more serious example of metaphor compounding an error of perception of Darwin's great theory.

As David J. Buller points out in his article from *Scientific American,* "Evolution of the Mind: 4 Fallacies of Psychology", Darwin did not make much use of the phrase "survival of the fittest". In fact, it was Herbert Spencer who first used this description when describing Darwin's work. Wallace, co-discoverer of Darwinian evolution, proposed that "survival of the fittest" may be an apt description. Darwin himself tended to put more emphasis on cooperation. "Tribes of moral men have an immense advantage over fractious bands of pirates", he once said. Huxley, known as Darwin's bulldog, promoted the gladiatorial view of evolution, talking about how the "strongest, swiftest and most cunning live to fight another day". So, the idea of nature being "red in tooth and claw", along with metaphors such as "it's a jungle out there", or "dog eat dog" crept into popular parlance. That's "nature", that's how "evolution" works, it's "survival of the fittest" it's "how the world works". No doubt when Jeff Shilling ran Enron he would say, "It's not me, I didn't invent 'survival of the fittest'. It is just the way of life. It's how we get progress". And so he implemented the system of rank and yank, of extreme competition within Enron.

The rather unpleasant idea of eugenics also grew out of a misunderstanding of Darwin's ideas.

Moving away from Darwin, the man often known as the guru on the metaphor is George Lakoff. In the book he co-wrote with Mark Johnson, *Metaphors We Live By*, it is argued that the metaphor is more than a figure of speech. It is literal. Take arguments, for example. When we speak about debate, metaphors for war become commonplace. "He attacked every weak point in my argument", or "I demolished his case" or "you disagree, OK shoot". Lagoff said that if we used metaphors that associated debate with a different activity, perhaps dance, then the result may be different and we may get a different concept of the term. We might find ourselves living in a less combative society.

Take the UK parliament. The two armies line up on opposite sides of the divide. Tories baying, Labour jeering. Instead, if we borrow the metaphor of dancing to describe political debate, we would describe Labour, Tories and the Liberals "taking their place on the floor". Cameron would waltz us through his idea for public sector cuts, with Miliband a step behind, wanting longer to reduce the structural deficit. Clegg would jive in his ideas for immigration, Balls responding with a jitterbug of his own.

Lagoff also talks about love as a journey: "our relationship has hit a dead end" or "I"m thinking of bailing out". In fact, our usage of the metaphor is so common we don't even realise we are doing it. Sure it can help advance understanding, maybe even underpin the march of civilisation, but metaphors can also make slaves of us.

Here are some examples of metaphors that we use which may prejudice us along a given line of reasoning: "Here comes the science bit". Translation: science is for geeks. "Property ladder", "safe as houses," "bricks and mortar". Translation: investing in property is safe, and prices can only go up. "Efficient market hypothesis"? That one speaks for itself.

Then there's "equilibrium": economists seem to be obsessed with this concept. They construct numerous models with equilibrium as the core requirement, but does it ever really exist? Isaac Newton's theories showed a universe following set rules. The universe seemed predictable. Pierre-Simon, Marquis de Laplace, a French mathematician and astronomer, thought of the concept of a demon to illustrate this idea of Newtonian predictability. Armed with information on the precise position of every particular in the cosmos, the Laplace demon could predict everything that will ever happen, and tell us about everything that had ever happened. We now believe that at the sub-molecular level, the universe is random. One cannot predict which hydrogen atoms will link with which oxygen atom to form water. Pour milk into coffee, you can predict it will diffuse, but not declare which atoms will end up in what place. Stephen Hawking in a piece entitled *Does God Play Dice?* takes it a step further: he states that black holes mean the universe is fundamentally random. "Information will be lost from our region of the universe," says Hawking "when black holes are formed, and then evaporate. This loss of information will mean that we can predict even less than we thought, on the basis of quantum theory. In quantum theory, one may not be able to predict with certainty, both the position, and the speed of a particle. But there is still one combination of position and speed that can be predicted. In the case of a black hole, this definite prediction involves both members of a particle pair. But, we can measure only the particle that comes out. There's no way even in principle that we can measure the particle that falls into the hole."

Even though our understanding of physics has changed enormously since Newton, economics still draws upon the pre-Einstein era of science, when such theses as the Heisenberg Uncertainty Principle hadn't been presented.[19] However, economists had already been seduced by the equilibrium metaphor. They produce all those diagrams showing demand, supply and marginal utility, and become so pre-occupied with making facts fit their metaphor that it never seems to occur to them the metaphor is wrong. George Soros turned on the topic of equilibrium rationality, perfect expectation and efficient markets in a speech back in April 1994. He said "It may seem strange that a patently false theory should gain such widespread acceptance." But, when you factor in that economists had become slaves to the metaphor, this needs no further explanation. Economists also fall for the metaphor that their subject is a science. It's kind of snobbery of the metaphor.[20] This is a shame: if they spent more time in the arts faculty, economists may have done a much better job of predicting the financial crises by studying history.

Here are some examples of metaphor: "Can't teach an old dog new tricks", meaning the old are stuck in their ways. "Clicks and mortar", used during the dotcom boom, to try and suggest some dotcoms were as safe as houses. When dotcoms crashed, the strength of that metaphor was such that people migrated from "clicks and mortar" to "bricks and mortar", which were seen as much safer. The result? We channelled our money into property that didn't produce wealth, avoided investments into assets that had the possibility to support innovation and, in doing so, sowed the seeds for the next crisis.

Tales, Tall Tales

Words matter. Language is a form of social grooming. Metaphors light up hard-to-grasp concepts but they have the power to enslave us. Here is another application of language that can lock the network together: the story.

We all love a good story, "A long time ago, in a galaxy far, far away", "No one can hear you scream", "Even when you thought it was safe to go back into the water." The ancients used to gather around the fire telling stories

---

[19] *When we try to measure something at the molecular level, the very act of measuring it changes the object in question*

[20] "I am a scientist, not an artist", says the economist

about their ancestors, and of the gods who existed in the natural world that surrounded them. If language provides social glue, can there be a better example of this in action than the story? In their book *Animal Spirits*, George Akerlof and Robert Shiller suggest that stories influence much of our thinking. They may even shape the direction of economics and underpin bubbles. Somehow, when a concept is expressed in terms of a story it has resonance that seems to strike us deep within our subconscious. "The emperor has no clothes." "Are scientists crying wolf over global warming?"

No wonder Christ resorted to parables to make his point.

Government ministers, leaders and academics often tell tales. CEOs sell a story to their shareholders. If enough variations of a story are told, it becomes a truth. Zeus cropped up time and time again in Greek mythology: therefore Zeus surely existed. Shiller and Akerloff tell how Mexican President Lopez Portillo told his people that Mexico was rich: they had struck oil. So convincing was Portillo's yarn that the country gave foreign aid to other South and Central American economies. The Pope visited in 1979, seemingly confirming Mexico was a global player of considerable importance. The country borrowed against future oil revenue. Alas, there was a lot less oil than originally thought, but who wanted to contradict the tale? Mexico, its leader and its populace were seduced by the story; the nation was left with a legacy of debt, inflation and resulting economic disaster.

Stories can inspire, but they can also mislead. "Son," said the old man to his youngest, now starting out in the world, "Take my advice. Buy a property as soon as you can. House prices only go up. Your mortgage gets cheaper every year. Trust me, you won't regret it. That's the story of my life: I bought my first house in 1967 and it set me back a fortune. £6,000 it cost me. Do you know that house is now worth £400,000?" The story we build up becomes all-powerful.

Tests using MRI show that when we hear a story the same area of the brain lights up as when we experience those events in reality. The key seems to be what are called "mirror neurons". This applies to chimps too: a chimp watches another chimp having a certain experience, and the same neurons in the two chimps are seen to fire. Writing for *New Scientist* magazine

Jessica Marshall says that it is possible that "... stories act as social glue binding people together in a common identity that is forged as they share the ideas or emotions prompted by narrative."

And so that's the story of glue. We are locked so tightly within the network that it is hard for us to question it. Our language and stories, our popular sayings, metaphors, and religion lock us into the network. Whilst not always bad, this is dangerous, by making us blind to the assumptions, the behaviours and the beliefs that can harm us.

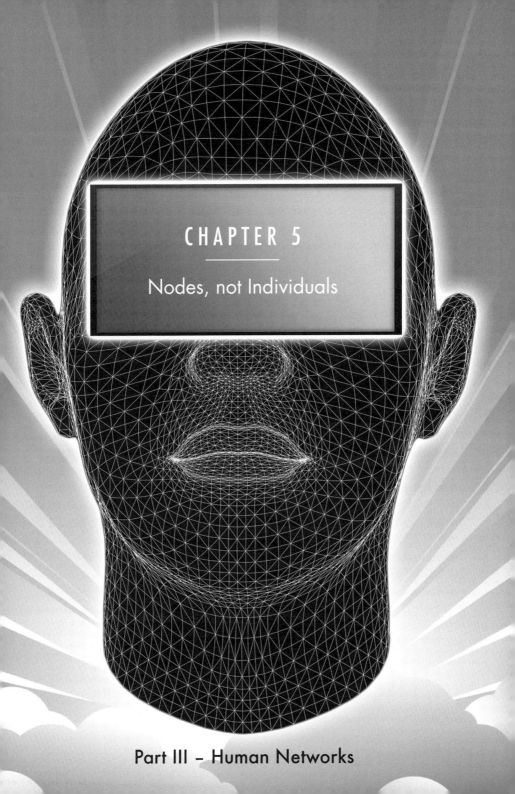

CHAPTER 5

Nodes, not Individuals

Part III – Human Networks

CHAPTER 5

Nodes, not Individuals

Economists give themselves airs. Perhaps the most accurate words ever uttered by an economist came from J.K. Galbraith when he said: "The only function of economic forecasting is to make astrology look respectable." The former Bank of England rate setter, Charles Goodhart, put economists in their place when he said: "As soon as the government attempts to regulate any particular set of financial assets, these become unreliable as indicators of economic trends."[21]

Perhaps this story, which I am told is true, says all that needs to be said on the subject.

When Einstein died, he arrived at the Pearly Gates with three other men. He looked at the first, and asked: "What's your IQ?" "180," came the reply, to which Einstein said: "Excellent! We can discuss my Theory of Relativity." To the second, he posed the same question and was met with the response: "160". "Good," said Einstein, "we can discuss the science of nuclear fusion." The third looked embarrassed. "My IQ is 80," he volunteered, to which Einstein replied: "And what's your forecast for the economy?"

Lord Keynes once said, "The ideas of economists and political philosophers, both when they are right and when they are wrong, are more powerful than is commonly understood. Indeed the world is ruled by little else. Practical men, who believe themselves to be quite exempt from any intellectual influence are usually the slaves of some defunct economist. Madmen in authority, who hear voices in the air, are distilling their frenzy from some academic scribbler of a few years back. I am sure that the power of vested interests is vastly exaggerated compared with the gradual encroachment of ideas."

---

[21] President Reagan once said, "An economist is someone who, on being shown something works in practice, wonders if it will work in theory." Churchill often had a sharp witticism to share. As Chancellor, he encapsulated economists (and in particular his advisor, arguably the greatest economist of the 20th century) in a handful of words saying: "When you get two economists in a room you get two opinions, unless one of them is Lord Keynes, in which case you get three opinions."

In reality, I suspect Keynes was wrong. Instead, it would be more accurate to say: "The network, both when it is right and when it is wrong, is more powerful than is commonly understood. Indeed the world is ruled by little else. Practical men, political thinkers and the economists who believe themselves to be at the forefront of original thought are usually the slaves of the nodes, hubs and connections in the network that surrounds them."

Culture from Economists, or Economists from Culture?

Economists are like flotsam and jetsam. Their culture and the circumstances of their era drive them and push them this way and that. When, on occasion, the forces beyond their control push them in a direction that makes it appear that they have stumbled onto something clever, they call out in celebration, and demand a Nobel Prize. The ancient Greeks called it "hubris". Should we act as if we are gods, we will surely fail. Icarus, wearing wings of feathers fastened together with wax, flew with his father across the heavens. Despite the advice he had received from Daedalus, ambition took him higher and higher, until he flew too close to the sun. The wax melted, causing him to fall to his death.

Here are two examples of economic hubris: central bankers and the economists who heap praise upon them.

During the first few years of the last decade, the economy seemed to be on a permanent trajectory of upward growth. At the same time, inflation stood firmly in check. Central bankers called this NICE (Non-Inflationary Consistently Expansionary), and they were given the credit for this miracle achievement. However, they were more circumspect in accepting this praise. Take Mervyn King, present Governor of the Bank of England. Contrary to Einstein's posthumous observations, he is a very clever man. A public display of patting one's own back? Not for Mervyn, surely.

He did, occasionally, let the veneer of humility slip. In May 2007 he told the Society of Business Economists: "The behaviour of the UK economy has improved over the past decade ... although structural reforms to the economy over several decades have made the economy better able to respond to economic shocks, the new monetary framework [that's the role taken by the Bank of England] has also played a key role." In 2004, Mr King said at the AEA annual conference, 2004: "The success of the American economy, and of the Federal Reserve in responding to the large economic and other shocks with which it has been confronted, is a tribute to Alan Greenspan and his colleagues."

Economists themselves were not so subtle. They heaped praise on both Mervyn King and Alan Greenspan. They didn't look so smart, however, when the financial crisis erupted. Even so, they managed to present innocent faces to the public. "Of course," went the gist of their defence, "what central bankers can do is quite limited." In other words, when times are good, it is down to savvy central bankers and clever economists but, where their achievement is shown to be an illusion, they rapidly point out that their ability to steer the economy is limited and that there are more powerful forces at work.

I agree with them: there are more powerful forces at work. The network that is the economy is too big and too complex for them to control. But, bankers and economists try to have it both ways, taking credit when things go well, absolving themselves of blame when things go badly.

In fairness to Alan Greenspan, in his book, *The Age of Turbulence,* he did say that the role of central bankers in creating economic stability is exaggerated. In fact, Mr Greenspan (or The Maestro, as he was once called) tried to warn us of these underlying forces at work. When he was chairman at the Fed he had confronted what he described as a paradox. The long-run rate of interest, as defined by the markets, fell below the short-run rate as determined by the central bank. History has shown us that when this happens it is a sign we are close to recession. But, at that point, no one was forecasting recession. Greenspan had maintained (and in fairness stated before the financial crisis broke out) that there are forces at work beyond the control of central banks. In fact, in part due to China's policy of maintaining a cheap currency, money was sloshing around the global banking system, meaning credit was both cheap and easy to come by. It is likely that this cheap credit would have been available regardless of the actions of central banks.

People criticise Greenspan for creating bubbles through allowing the build-up of the pressures that led to the financial crisis. However it is entirely possible that Greenspan was powerless throughout.

There are signs that when China finally relents and allows her currency to appreciate, we may see the opposite circumstances and credit will be short in supply. At the same time, as they begin to retire, baby boomers across the developed world will draw down on savings. Simultaneously demand for investment across emerging economies will rise. The combination of all these developments may lead to much higher real interest rates across the world, regardless of what central banks do.[22]

Society hates it when people in power say "I don't know" or "There is not much I can do." Back in 1988, at a speech to the Economic Club of New York, Alan Greenspan famously said: "I guess I should warn you, if I turn out to be particularly clear, you've probably misunderstood what I've said." Personally, I took that to be a confession that The Maestro, to put it politely, was subtly inferring that: "I'm making this up as I go along." Even so, the world looked on in wonder. "How clever Greenspan is," they cried. His successor at the Fed, Ben Bernanke, promised to come clean if he wasn't sure what was going on. He was pilloried in the media and by the markets for his honesty; they felt he was indecisive. For my money, Greenspan hid uncertainly behind a veneer of confidence or, so brazen was he in his nakedness, that people believed that he was fully clothed. Conversely, when Bernanke said: "I will come clean: I forgot to get dressed this morning," everyone jeered.

Keynes, The Myth of the Demigod

Take another example of such a very clever economist not being quite as radical as we believe. I am not, for one moment, positing that Keynes wasn't intelligent. He was extremely so, perhaps the brainiest man in Britain throughout the entire course of the first half of the last century. But his radicalism wasn't so radical. Keynes was a child of his time; not its father, as some might like to think.

Keynes was one of the first macroeconomists. As such, his views coincide with one of the main hypotheses of this book: a network, such as the economy, is more than the sum of its parts. In his famous General Theory

---

[22] McKinsay Global, looked at the possibility that a shortage of savings relative to demand for investment could lead to higher real interest rates across the world at the tail end of 2010. I thought it was one of the most important economic reports I had read in a long time.

of Employment, Interest and Money, published in 1936, he argued that under certain conditions, what was right for the individual (such as saving during a recession) was wrong for the economy. He advocated a number of policy responses to be implemented in times of severe recession. But did he really invent Keynesian economics? For one thing, there was considerable overlap between the theories of Keynes and the Austrian economist Joseph Schumpeter.[23] For another, Keynesian economics had already been tried. The New Deal, introduced by the Franklin Delano Roosevelt government in the 1930s, was a form of Keynesian stimulus launched before Keynes' general theory was published. Although the New Deal Mark II may have been influenced by Keynes, as far as I am aware no one has claimed that this was the case for the first phase.[24]

When Keynes died and the discipline of economics that inherited his name entered the mainstream, it was hijacked by other economists. So much so, that if he had lived to see the day, he himself may not have described himself as a Keynesian.[25]

The economic policies of the 1950s, 1960s and early 1970s fitted the social mood of that era. After the Second World War, there was dissatisfaction both with the old way of doing things, as well as with the elites responsible for taking us into two world wars. People like the fictional Captain Mainwaring saw themselves as self-made men having bettered themselves by the sweat of their brow, while the former elite, symbolised by failed ex-public school boy Sergeant Wilson, tried to live off their class and their former glories. In this context, Keynesian economics felt right.

As for Keynes himself, his influences (without which his theory would surely have never seen the light of the day) included the harsh economic backdrop of the time. This zeitgeist also drew upon his own close circle of intellectual

---

[23] Arthur Smithies, in a paper entitled "Schumpeter and Keynes" from *The Review of Economics and Statistics*, and Peter F. Drucker, *Modern Prophets: Schumpeter or Keynes*, both produced good reviews, comparing Schumpeter and Keynes.

[24] Robert B. Reich, in an article for *Time Magazine* provided an excellent, easy-to-read summary of Keynes, including his relationship with Franklin D. Roosevelt.

[25] Tim Congdon, *Keynes, the Keynesians and Monetarism*, made a good investigation into the question was Keynes a Keynesian?

friends in the Bloomsbury Group, including both Virginia Woolf and E. M. Forster. Keynes may be considered a mover and shaker but, I submit, he himself was moved and shaken by the network that surrounded him. If there had been no Keynes, I am sure someone else would have invented Keynesian economics. It may not have been called that of course, but it would have smelled as sweet.

Mr R & Mrs T

In more recent history, Margaret Thatcher, the Iron Lady, applied the economics of the housewife to UK plc. Just like families, she argued, the UK must live within its means. Out went Keynesianism; in came the ideas of Milton Friedman, Friedrich Hayek and Alan Walters. In a way it was the death of macroeconomics, or network theory, as applied to the economy.

Did economists and politicians such as Mrs Thatcher and her US counterpart Ronald Reagan change the political landscape? Was this proof that political thinkers shaped the world as Keynes said? No it wasn't.

Read these words: "We used to think that you could spend your way out of a recession and increase employment by cutting taxes and boosting government spending. I tell you in all candour that that option no longer exists and, insofar as it ever did exist, it only worked on each occasion since the war by injecting a bigger dose of inflation into the economy, followed by a higher level of unemployment as the next step." This was pure monetarist economics; Thatcher at her most extreme. Except, that Britain's first woman Prime Minister was not responsible for that statement. They were spoken by James Callaghan, the leader of the Labour party, Prime Minister before Thatcher, at a Labour Party Conference in 1976.

The country moved away from Keynesianism to a more old-fashioned, market-based model because the mood of the network demanded it. The system had apparently thrown out the ideas of Keynes; the electorate wanted a new approach.

Efficient Markets, Filthy Rich

If you take Thatcherism or Reaganomics to the extreme, you end up with the tyranny of the markets. Economists, the children of the Thatcher revolution, dreamt up such esoteric ideas as the "efficient market hypothesis" (the idea that markets and economic agents, you and me, have perfect knowledge and are 100 per cent rational), or invent extraordinary theories such as the Black–Scholes model, which is supposed to reduce market dynamics to mathematical formulae that make trading more profitable and scientific. In the 1990s we were told that the 1980s stood for greed and that era was dead; that Gordon Gekko was in the past; that characters such as Harry Enfield's "Loadsamoney" were an anachronism. And yet, Labour heavyweight Peter Mandelson, future right-hand man to Gordon Brown, said in 1998 during that decade of enlightenment when we were no longer greedy: "We are intensely relaxed about people getting filthy rich."

In fact, Mr Mandelson added "as long as they pay their taxes." But, the ethos of the 1980s: the philosophy of Thatcherism as moulded by the failure of Keynesianism, as formed by a Great Depression and the social upheaval that came with two world wars, was that greed was good. Yet in 1998 that idea was still strong.

New idealism or new economic thinking could not shake that philosophy. During the boom years of the noughties, plenty warned that all that greed and debt would come to no good. But, these voices were ignored. The IMF, which is supposed to take a more global, holistic view of the economy was, by its very own admission, (according to an IEO report, "IMF Performance in the Run-Up to the Financial and Economic Crisis") guilty of groupthink. It took the biggest financial crisis in almost a century, an economy close to collapse, and talk that capitalism itself was on its knees to change the deeply embedded views of a generation of politicians, economists and their electorate.

The two greatest sideshows to the economic crisis, namely MP's expense claims and banker greed, were symptoms of that era. They did not cause it. They were caused by it.

The network tying ideas together is all pervasive. Even the hubs, people like Keynes or Reagan or Thatcher, are the products of deeper forces. They do not mould the connections that pass through them. In fact, they are moulded by them and their influence can only be allowed to spread if the network accepts them.

Ideas, Patents, No Ideas

It is not just economists who are slaves to the network and culture of their time. The men and women who are supposedly our most innovative may be similarly limited; this limitation is not necessarily a bad thing, but it exists nonetheless. It is important that we acknowledge it.

For example, take patents. Surely the introduction of patents has underpinned innovation. Or has it? If the hypothesis for this chapter is correct, then patents may actually be a hindrance, and may stand in the way of creating greater collective wealth.

Take the brilliant mathematician, Gottfried Leibniz. The unfortunate fellow was a towering figure in German intellectual life during the latter years of the 18th and early 19th centuries. It could be argued that he made one of the most important discoveries of all time. He also played an important role in helping a certain Georg Ludwig ascend to the rank of King George I of England. And yet, when Leibniz died, the English King (who happened to be in the region at the time) pointedly refused to attend the funeral. His grave remained unmarked for 50 years. Why such an ignominious end for such a brilliant man?

It seems his error was to have had the gall to have made the claim that he had discovered calculus, for Isaac Newton had made the very same claim. The English King could not been seen to offer any kind of favour, either in life or afterwards, to the man who had posed a threat to the darling of the English intelligentsia. So, poor old Gottfried became embroiled in a row with the man who would always gain sway over the people who mattered at that time.

Actually, it is possible the row was meaningless. Surely it was Archimedes who really discovered calculus? He may not have defined it to the nth degree, but he laid the foundations, so that the likes of Newton and Leibniz had to do little more than put the pieces together. The point of the story is not so much to clarify that Newton was something of a bully (true nonetheless), but rather that even Newton, irrespective of his brilliance, was himself a product of the network that surrounded him. He grew up in an age of mathematical reasoning, when the boundaries of mathematics were expanding.[26]

The tale of Newton and Leibniz is not an isolated event. The history of innovation is bubbling over with examples of the coincidence of simultaneous discovery.

Were logarithms discovered by John Napier and Henry Briggs or by the Swiss mathematician, Jobst Bürgi? Alas, for Bürgi it seems his shade can make a credible case for claiming the invention, but the 30 Years War reduced his work to virtual anonymity. It was in Britain where a Scot (Napier) and an Englishman (Briggs) collaborated to advance our knowledge of logs. There wasn't much in it: Bürgi's work was published in 1619, Briggs published *Logarithmorum Chilias Prima* in 1617, a few months after Napier's death. However, there is evidence to suggest Bürgi's work began first. Nonetheless, what is fairly clear is that the two Brits worked independently of Bürgi, largely ignorant of his existence.[27]

The list of so called coincidences runs on. Sunspots were discovered by four different scientists, each living in a different country, in 1611. Molecular theory was invented independently in 1811 and 1814. In 1869, the Frenchmen Louis Arthur Ducos du Hauron and Charles Cros independently invented colour photography. Joseph Swan demonstrated an incandescent light bulb in Britain in 1878; Edison patented his lamp in 1879.[28]

The list continues ...

Darwin discovered evolution, but only up to a point. In fact, Alfred Russell Wallace is credited with having co-discovered evolution. Darwin thought of it first, but was so spooked by his findings and the backlash he knew it would cause that he sat on his ideas for years. When he discovered that Wallace

---

[26] The conflict between Newton and Leibniz was told well by Anand Kandaswamy, *The Newton/ Leibniz Conflict in Context* and Alfred Rupert Hall, *Philosophers at War: The Quarrel between Newton and Leibniz*

[27] Steven Johnson, *Where Good ideas come from* provides a good account of coincidences in discovery, including the story of logarithms, and the discovery of sun spots

[28] See previous footnote

had independently stumbled onto an almost identical theory, he rushed out the publication of his work, and agreed with Wallace for the two papers to be published on the same day. But, while Darwin's work drew inspiration from the Galapagos Islands, he was not similarly isolated. Rather, Darwin grew up in an era when botany was a subject of great debate.

Carl Linnaeus, the man who is known as the father of taxonomy, was born just short of a hundred years before Darwin was born. Other influences on Darwin included Charles Lyell, the author of *Principles of Geology*, in which he asserted that the Earth was shaped by slow moving forces, and Jean-Baptiste Lamarck, known for his work on inheritance of acquired characteristics. Most famously of all, Thomas Malthus, an economist, advanced the idea that increase in population will always outpace productivity and growth, such that starvation will surely result. It was Malthus' ideas that focused Darwin on seeing life as a constant struggle. Darwin said, after reading Malthus "it at once struck me that under these circumstances variations would tend to be preserved and unfavourable ones destroyed." In fact, Charles Darwin wasn't the only member of his family to work on the pioneering edge of botany. His very own grandfather, Erasmus Darwin was, in his day, one of the leading figures in the world on this discipline.[29]

It seems it is the network, not individuals working alone, that provides the oxygen for innovation. Indeed, the network itself led to the discovery of oxygen, with Priestley and Scheele clashing over who should have earned the credit.[30]

Even the great innovations that underpinned the Industrial Revolution are attributable to networks. The history books that describe the era list a handful of men, for example John Kay and his flying shuttle or James Hargreaves and the spinning jenny. However, the history books provide a distorted view. The reality, as Terence Kealey points out in his book *Sex, Science and Profits*, is that it was an army of labourers and engineers, working together, who made small changes here and there. (See also *Negotiating the Rewards of Invention: The Shop-Floor Inventor in Victorian Britain Business History* by Christine Macleod.) It is a myth that the Industrial Revolution saw a number of discrete steps. Kealey supports this proposition by quoting Robert

---

[29] Autobiography of Charles Darwin

[30] The classic study investigating the coincidence of discoveries was William F. Ogburn and Dorothy Thomas, *Are Inventions Inevitable? A Note on Social Evolution* back in 1922.

Stephenson who said: "The locomotive is not the invention of one man but of a nation of engineers," and the industrialist, A. J. Mundella, who said: "Every invention we have made and patented (and some have created almost a revolution in the trade) has been the invention of overlookers, or ordinary working men, or skilled mechanics, in every instance."

So, if innovations are down to the network, why do individuals get the credit? And how do these individuals manage to patent ideas which were generated by collaboration? Terence Kealey argues that patents have been a hindrance to innovation. He cited Henry Ford, whose efforts to mass produce the motor car were held back by a patent held by the Association of Licensed Automobile Manufacturers. Or, consider the development of flight, which was apparently hindered by patents held by the Wright Brothers. They slapped writs on other aviators so frequently that the whole industry nearly failed to take off.[31]

Octopus, Networks and the Shade

The network pervades culture in other ways. Take, as an example, the most important band in the history of popular and rock music. I think a credible argument can be made for saying the Beatles and its four members are up there with Mozart and Beethoven in terms of their influence on music. Yet, what if there had been no band? What if John Lennon's first group, The Quarrymen, had remained intact? What if Lennon had sent Paul McCartney away with a flea in his ear, instead of allowing him to join the band? What would have happened in the history of rock and roll?

Clearly, both men were enormously talented, although I believe that if there had been no connection, neither would have had even a pale copy of the

---

[31] Andrew Goldberg said in his article 'Patent defendants aren't copycats. So who's the real inventor here?' "One big difference between patents and other kinds of intellectual property, like copyrights and trademarks, is that patent-holders who want to sue someone for infringement don't have to show that their patents or their products were actually copied by the defendant. In fact, the issue of copying is legally irrelevant when determining whether or not someone infringed a patent. (It is relevant to wilfulness—more on that below.) The flip side of that rule is that a defendant company can have a really nice story about they did their own research, invention, and development—but it doesn't matter one bit, legally speaking. Such 'independent invention' stories are no defense." He went on to quote studies from Mark Lemley (Stanford) and Christopher Cotropia (U. of Richmond) – Copying in Patent Law and said: "The researchers studied 193 patent cases and found only 21 of them – that's 10.9 per cent – that contained even an allegation of any copying, whether that's copying from a patent or from a patent-holder's commercial product."

careers that they enjoyed. Perhaps Lennon would still be alive. I can imagine him being cited as a bit player in the story of the Rolling Stones. Perhaps he might have penned a great hit for the Kinks. Maybe he would have been a writer for the TV show, *The Monkees*. It is quite interesting to speculate what this alternative reality, one in which there had been no Beatles, would be like.

I suspect, however, that things would have been not so different. The 1960s would still have been a decade of great change. Rock and Roll would have still developed. The Stones, the Kinks, Pink Floyd, Led Zeppelin and David Bowie would have still existed, although their songs and names may have been slightly different. The most influential band in history was probably not quite as influential as we think. In fact, I put to you that in the vacuum that would have been left had the Beatles not emerged, another star, another group of musical geniuses, would have taken their place.

If you really want to point to an event that triggered the evolution of rock and roll, you will probably be disappointed. There was no event. However, the slave trade was the key historical development. With this trade, and the eventual emancipation of slaves, we saw two cultures meet and, in the reaction that occurred, music changed. Western styles, with their roots in musical structure and mathematical precision, mixed with African music, with its greater emphasis on rhythm. What we see looking back, are two networks merging. This is otherwise known as cross-fertilisation. Bill Haley, Little Richard, Buddy Holly, Elvis Presley and the Beatles were the result. Legend has it that rock and roll was invented when blues singer Robert Johnson made a pact with the Devil. It is said he met Satan at the intersection of Highways 49 and 61 in Clarksdale, Mississippi, and in that meeting he went from being the "worst guitarist to the best guitarist". In reality, the devil was simply in the detail of a step-by-step evolution, set off by the merging of two networks. Even the Beatles were, by contrast, little more than bit players.

The connections created were not limited to two men; the sublime talent did not solely belong to Lennon and McCartney. Frank Sinatra has said his favourite Lennon and McCartney song was *Something*. It is not hard to see why, for this was indeed a beautiful song, but written by George Harrison. *An Octopus's Garden*, may not be the Beatles' greatest work of genius, but equally, it has proved to be a pretty memorable tune. Yet this song was written by Ringo Starr.

It is surely stretching credibility to say it is only coincidence that four such fine song-writers all knew each other as kids.[32] The coincidence of their shared background is an inadequate explanation. It is clearly the case that they complemented each other, and in turn fed off each other, enhancing one another's ability. Had McCartney not met Lennon, had Harrison gone to a different school, had Richard Starkey stayed with his previous band (Rory Storm and the Hurricanes) had George Martin got his wish and recruited a different drummer altogether, those crucial connections in the network would never had been formed.

We would still have rock and roll; all of the band members would have enjoyed successful careers, but I suspect they would have never attained anything like the celebrity status that they had.

---

[32] That's not entirely how it happened. True, McCartney and Harrison went to the same school, McCartney met Lennon at a garden fete. Starr was a well-known drummer in Liverpool.

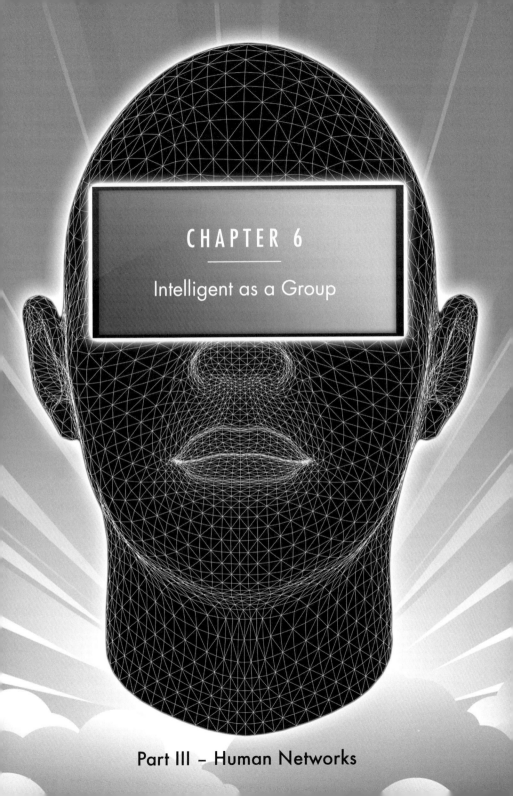

CHAPTER 6

Intelligent as a Group

Part III – Human Networks

CHAPTER 6

Intelligent as a Group

Crowds can be capable of great insights. Indeed, our progress, if progress is what you want to call it, has been charged by the crowd. The mechanism of technology, from how to make fire, tame horses and land on the moon has been fashioned by the crowd. As new technology emerges that makes it easier for the crowd to communicate, as we are enabled to communicate in much larger groups, the speed with which we innovate accelerates. The focus now is on the intelligence of the crowd and, to take a positive perspective, there are good reasons to believe the network of humanity is becoming much smarter.

The Wisdom of the Crowd

Crowds can be very intelligent. The classic experiment that allegedly proves their wisdom dates back to 1906, when Francis Galton attended a livestock fair, where villagers were asked to guess the weight of an ox on display. Galton, who was something of a numbers man, closely associated with a handful of theories in the field of statistics, noticed that not a single guess was right. Yet, when he took the mean of all attempts, it was remarkably close.[33] The story of Galton, and the idea of wisdom of crowds is told by James Surowiecki in *The Wisdom of Crowds: Why the Many Are Smarter Than the Few and How Collective Wisdom Shapes Business, Economies, Societies and Nations.*

Another example of wisdom of the crowds is provided by the TV show *Who Wants to be a Millionaire?*, where contestants can choose to "ask the audience". However, the audience does not always get it right. This is particularly true if the subject matter is quite obscure, or if it is worded in such a way that the instinctive answer is wrong.

Consider this situation: there are three cannibals and three missionaries standing together on the bank of a river. They need to get across the river.

---

[33] The ox weighed 1198 pounds, and of the 800 or so guesses, the mean average was 1197 pounds.

They have one boat, which can only hold two people. At no point can the cannibals on either side of the river outnumber the missionaries, or the one will become the other's lunch. How many trips will it take to get all six of the people safely across the river? It's not that tricky, as puzzles go. Back in 1932, Marjorie Shaw from Columbia University in her study "Comparison of Individuals and Small Groups in the Rational Solution of Complex Problems" put this puzzle, along with several others to both individuals and small groups of four people. The groups were more successful in solving the puzzles.

According to J. C. Glick and K. Staley (2007) a small group of doctors, working together as a team, are more likely to make an accurate diagnosis than working alone; college students sitting examinations perform better when students work together than when working individually. So compelling is the evidence to support the idea that students perform better when they work in groups, a number of universities have started implementing what has become known as "collaborative learning techniques;" as was stated by William Breedlove, Tracy Burkett and Idee Winfield, in "Collaborative Testing and Test Performance" (2004).

Cross-fertilisation: My Ideas from Your Ideas

On other occasions, we become smarter when different networks collide. When African music with its traditions in rhythm collided with more regulated European music, something different was created.

Or, when the innovation known as the packaged holiday took off, Brits discovered new cultures, and slowly became open to new styles of cuisine. The British palate, for so long the joke of Europe, changed dramatically. The rise of Indian restaurants is a good example. At first, these restaurants were popular because in Britain during the 1970s and early 1980s there was very little to do once the pubs shut. So, a trip to the curry house proved to be a cheap and popular way to extend the evening. At first, the cuisine provided by these restaurants must have provided quite a shock to the conservative British palate: Indian food has flavour. To begin with, the food provided was fairly simple when compared with Indian restaurants of today. So, at first, the Indian restaurants largely catered for the desire to stay out later. Over time the British palate changed, and began to appreciate international flavour. Today, Indian restaurants are popular because they provide food people like; what is notable is that their menus are quite different from those available from restaurants in India. In the world of ideas, innovation occurs when those of different backgrounds share their knowledge and merge ideas from two different disciplines.

The printing press changed the world. As I will discuss later in this chapter, it was one of the four most important innovations of all time. It was invented by cobbling together ideas from different industries perhaps even from different continents. As Steven Johnson points out in *Where Good Ideas Come From*, Gutenberg himself was a goldsmith. And yet, his invention came by modifying the wine presses used by vintners. In fact, it is possible (although by no means certain) that he got wind of the Chinese system of printing, which had not been adapted for the mass production of texts.

But, if the printing press underpinned innovation, the discovery of DNA gave us new and deeper understanding. The double-helix structure of DNA was identified when Francis Crick and James Watson built experiments on x-rays supplied by the biochemist Rosalind Franklin using "… tools from multi-disciplines: biochemistry, genetics, information theory, and mathematics," or so says Steven Johnson.[34] In turn, the physicist George Gamow studied the work of Watson and Crick and, drawing upon the knowledge of his own discipline, explained how the four bases in the double helix of DNA could control the synthesis of protein from amino acids.[35] Johnson quotes Arthur Koestler who, in his book *The Act of Creation*, says all decisive events in the history of scientific thought can be described in terms of cross-fertilisation between different disciplines.

John Stuart Mill was equally perceptive when he said "It is hardly possible to overrate the value … of placing human beings in contact with persons dissimilar to themselves, with modes of thought and action unlike those with which they are familiar."

As previously discussed, the discipline of economics has been greatly influenced by physics. The French physicist Marie-Esprit-Léon Walras, often called the Father of Equilibrium, laid down many of the foundation stones of microeconomic theory. But, he drew heavily from the ideas of physicists

---

[34] *Where good ideas come from* page 168.

[35] http://en.wikipedia.org/wiki/George_Gamow

of that time. One of the problems with economic thought is that it became stuck in the mud. As concepts such as the Second Law of Thermodynamics, quantum theory and ideas such as Heisenberg's Uncertainty Principle were developed, economics stayed with its original tools. Just as Newton failed to interpret the underlying economics of the South Sea Bubble, economics itself failed to move on from Newton.

Today, we are seeing cross-fertilisation between economics and biology, with a good deal of psychology thrown in. With that, the discipline has become more interesting, and seems to be much closer to building a credible model of the economy. Network theory is itself an example of such cross-fertilisation. Much of the original work in this field was carried out by physicists. Today it is being applied across the spectrum to biology, economics, demographics, chemistry, neurology and psychology.

The Internet represents an extraordinary mechanism for cross-fertilisation.

The Spice of Variety

The idea that cross-fertilisation is crucial to innovation and can lead to economic change is closely linked to the role played by luck.

Ideas developed for one purpose can, by chance, prove to be relevant to others. Evolutionary scientists refer to this as "exaptation". So, for example, the ancestors of birds developed feathers used for heat regulation. These feathers were later adapted for flight. Early hominids may have learned to walk on two legs for a given purpose (scientists are not entirely sure why), but later on found that having two arms free afforded evolutionary benefits to those who were that little bit smarter. So, because we have two arms and two legs, we began to become more intelligent. [36]

Is that really luck? It may be more accurate to say innovation needs variety. If you try enough ideas, you will eventually succeed. Innovation is at least partly a random process. For new ideas, new discoveries, or a change in attitude to take place we need variety. For, in that way, we are more likely to take the next great step forward. Steven Johnson quotes the economist William Stanley Jevons, who once said: "The errors of the great mind exceed in number those of the less vigorous."

---

[36] Richard Leakey, *The Origin of Humankind*

As R. W. Johnson, Jr., a former eponymous boss at Johnson & Johnson said: "Failure is our most important product". In other words, only through trial and improvement can one innovate.

In business there is a danger of being too focused. For individual countries this approach may make sense. But if companies stay too focused, they are less likely to be responsible for the next big idea. Back in September 2008, Nassim Taleb, (the author of *The Black Swan*) and David Shaywitz argued that drug companies were becoming too focused in their R&D, thereby eliminating the possibility of a chance discovery. They said: "Pharma companies have been trying to boost output by increasing efficiency, narrowing their focus to a handful of disease areas, shelving safe but ineffective compounds without fully exploring their scientific potential and trying to ensure that each project the company is working on is carried out with a clearly defined market segment in mind. So intent are managers on maintaining focus that important opportunities for novel discoveries are lost, as is the intellectual space for tinkering and capitalising on chance observations and unexpected directions so important in medical research."[37]

Four Excellent Innovations

There have been lots of innovations and discoveries that have changed the world. A case can be made for many of them as the single most important. Perhaps, it was the discovery of how to make fire which enabled us to cook meat, freeing up time so we did not have to wait so long to digest our food. It also promoted rituals, which may have helped add to social cohesion. Perhaps it was the wheel, or the domestication of animals. Perhaps it was a more recent innovation, such as the discovery of penicillin.

All these innovations, all these discoveries were important.

No one is an island. At least, in terms of advancing knowledge, no one is isolated. The great geniuses of the renaissance, De Vinci and Michelangelo fed off each other. They were children of the rebirth of learning. The most original minds were influenced by the network that surrounded them.

---

[37] Drugs research needs serendipity, *The Financial Times*, 29 July 2008

As such, I have highlighted four innovations that were vital for us in our development.

Strictly speaking, there were no discrete innovations at all. Every great step forward was actually a series of tiny steps. But, for the sake of simplicity and for the sake of ensuring this book isn't several thousand pages long, here are the big four innovations that stand out, at least in my mind.

First, there was the innovation called *speech*. Evidence suggests that our cousins, *Homo sapiens neanderthalensis*, were also capable of speech. Certainly tests of Neanderthal remains indicate that they too had the FOXP2 gene, associated with speech in humans (Alec MacAndrew, "FOXP2 and the Evolution of Language"). But, most seem to agree that for Neanderthals speech was not nearly as sophisticated. As I said above, there was no sudden breakthrough. One day, early man did not wake and suddenly find speech was his (or more likely hers), fully formed like Athena bursting from the head of Zeus.[38] In fact, speech would have developed gradually, over the ages. Having said that, it does not seem unreasonable to speculate that *Home sapiens'* "killer app", was speech, complete with grammar, and all the nuances that we are familiar with today. As was pointed out in Chapter 3, Robin Dunbar theorises that speech evolved because it enabled us to function in larger communities, of around 150 in size. What is so special about 150? What is the benefit to us in living in communities of around that size? It is surely the case that thanks to speech, collaboration took us to new levels of sophistication. You had tool-makers, tailors, soldiers and hunters; you had the shaman. Individuals could specialise, honing their own particular skill. There is evidence that early humans traded with each other (mentioned earlier), again providing evidence of cooperation over distances, something that would have been impossible without speech.

The point of this argument is not so much to suggest speech was vital. Of course it was. Speech was especially vital because it promoted cooperation. So powerful was this advance that it is quite remarkable that agriculture did not develop until so late in our evolution. Until, that is, you take into account that for much of the time *Homo sapiens* has been on Earth, we lived in an

---

[38] "I say hers, because it is has been speculated that speech began as communication between mother and child, and that only with the onset of monogamy, did males too begin to practice speech as adults." *Ape that spoke,* John McCrone

ice age: those conditions may have made it especially hard to farm. Then 15,000 years ago the Earth got suddenly warmer: archaeological evidence indicates that we rapidly became more sophisticated, and started to farm and trade. Then, the Younger Dryas, a kind of mini ice age, occurred; this must have substantially delayed the development of agriculture. Once this period ended, we progressed with remarkable speed.

Whether the move from hunter-gatherer to farmer-trader was a good thing in terms of promoting happiness is a moot point; such a development was inevitable once we had developed modern speech. All that was standing in our way was the climate.

So, assuming that progress is a good thing, speech was the key development in promoting it.

The next stage in our cultural development required an innovation for enhancing cooperation. Once we began to inhabit cities we lived in communities, which the nature of our evolution suggests was far from ideal. But, nonetheless, city dwelling took cooperation to new heights. The great cities of the Ancient World, whose discoveries and art really were quite something, began to take shape. There was Babylon, and its hanging gardens, the cities of the Middle East and then, much later, classical Athens. We had farmed for thousands of years and, by latter standards, progress was slow. The emergence of great cities made things change and progress or, if you prefer, evolution in its true meaning, accelerated.

But why? What was the development that enabled the emergence of these great cities? I submit it was the second great innovation: *writing*. Writing was not there at the outset of town dwelling. The early towns of the Levant developed before writing. The cities of the Aztecs and Incas did not have writing (although some evidence suggests this view may be wrong), but the great cities of the Ancient World in Mesopotamia, Egypt, the Indus Valley and China all had their own script. Like speech, it did not form overnight. To begin with, writing was primitive and used merely as a form of stock keeping. The first people to learn how to write were probably accountants.

With the fall of Rome in the West, and then of the China under the Song dynasty 1000 years later, progress slowed. In fact, in many respects, it went into something of a reversal.

But, in the West, cooperation and cross-fertilisation opened the door to a new era. Advances in shipping technology promoted trade over larger distances, the fall of Constantinople in 1453 saw learned scholars flee to Europe where their ideas mixed with the thinking of Medieval Christendom and the Crusades, although bloody, violent, and synonymous with hatred and intolerance in the Muslim world today, did at least introduce Western civilisation to a more sophisticated Islamic culture. Some scholars believe the Crusades and the cross-fertilisation they brought opened the way for the Renaissance.

The Renaissance, the Reformation and the Agrarian and Industrial Revolutions that followed occurred in relative quick succession. Another innovation took place during this period; its importance was great indeed. It was the next big thing, after speech and writing: it promoted a new level of cooperation. I refer to the *printing press*. Again, there was no discrete step. The Chinese had their own printing press before Gutenberg, perhaps independently, built his own. Fashioned around 1436, its main impact was not immediate. It is hard to say how important it was in promoting the Renaissance. However, the fact that Gutenberg managed to print a Bible probably demonstrates how important this technology was in advancing the Reformation.

Would the Industrial Revolution have occurred without the printing press? Many of the heroes of that revolution, James Watt, James Trevithick and George Stephenson were poorly educated. George Stephenson did not learn to write until he was 19, and never really did get maths.[39] These men were primarily practical: their heads were in machines, not in letters. But then again, the Industrial Revolution was not down to a few men: it was a nation of engineers, quietly beavering away; cooperating with one another, even if their cooperation was tacit. Without the printing press, I doubt whether that network of engineers, of ideas, would have ever reached sufficient critical mass for the Industrial Revolution to have occurred.

But, if there is a question mark over how important print was in charging the Industrial Revolution, there is surely no doubt as to how important it was in providing the ammunition for the remarkable period that followed. The years between 1867 and 1914 may have been the single most important half

---

[39] Terence Kealey, *Sex, Science and Profits* , page 179

century ever for the story of innovation. Smil Vaclav in his book *Creating the Twentieth Century* calls it the Age of Symmetry. The early years of this momentous era began with the discovery of dynamite, followed swiftly by the telephone and photographic film. The 1880s alone, says Vaclav, gave us "electricity – generating plants, electric motors, steam turbines, the gramophone, cars, aluminium production, air-filled rubber tires, and pre-stressed concrete." And, in the early 1900s we saw the first "airplanes, tractors, radio signals and plastics, neon lights and assembly line production." The printing press was surely the means by which the great discoverers of that period learnt their trade, learnt about the work of their contemporaries. It was the means by which collaboration was taken to new heights.

The 20th century did, of course, see impressive innovations but, by large, they were derivative ideas. The motor car, aeroplane, electricity, telephone and radio signals all saw big advances in application, but they were invented, or discovered before the First World War. But, slowly, and bit by bit, some of these technologies merged, cross-fertilisation between disciplines and industries took place, and a new innovation, an innovation that took collaboration to new heights, began to take shape.

This latest innovation is called the Internet.

There are ample studies out there which demonstrate the importance of the Internet in promoting innovation. Some Internet products act as a pool for enabling inventors to submit their ideas. Companies looking for solutions to problems now use the Internet to reach innovators previously inaccessible. Wikipedia and Linux demonstrate the power of collaboration. To give a simple example, one amongst thousands, consider the Open Prosthetics Project. In their own words: "The Open Prosthetics Project is producing useful innovations in the field of prosthetics and freely sharing the designs. This project is an open source collaboration between users, designers and financiers with the goal of making creations available for anyone to use and build upon. Our hope is to use this and our complementary sites to create a core group of 'lead users,' and to speed up and amplify the impact of their innovations in the industry."[40]

---

[40] The Open Prosthetics Project http://www.openprosthetics.org/

To take another example, look to the field of mathematics. Timothy Gowers, a professor of mathematics at Cambridge, has been experimenting on how collaboration through the Internet can lead to advances in the field of mathematics. He calls it the Polymath Project. In one experiment he focused on the Hales–Jewett Theorem. The experiment was described in the Institute of Advanced Study's (IAS) newsletter in the Autumn of 2010: it states "The problem Gowers posted sought an elementary proof of a special case of the density Hales–Jewett theorem. A little more than a month later, Gowers announced that the polymath participants – including Terence Tao, a Professor at the University of California, Los Angeles – had found an elementary proof of the special case that, surprisingly, could be generalized to prove the full theorem." The point of this anecdote is not to wax lyrical about the advances in the Hales–Jewett theorem, but to show how the Internet, via harnessing the power of collaboration and groupthink, can advance knowledge at a pace previously not considered possible. The IAS newsletter also stated: "Among the advantages of a collaborative online approach", said Gowers, "are the speed with which problems can be solved – in the case of the Hales–Jewett theorem, a matter of six weeks rather than several years – and the blog's working record of the mathematical process, showing how ideas grow, change, improve, or are discarded. In addition, different perspectives are encouraged and unanticipated connections are formed."[41]

If crowds can be smart, then technology can enable them to work closer together in ever larger groups. No technology, in the story of our species comes even close to matching the Internet for enabling crowds to cooperate. Thanks to this technology, the human network can become so very smart indeed.

[41] http://www.ias.edu/files/pdfs/letter-2010-fall.pdf

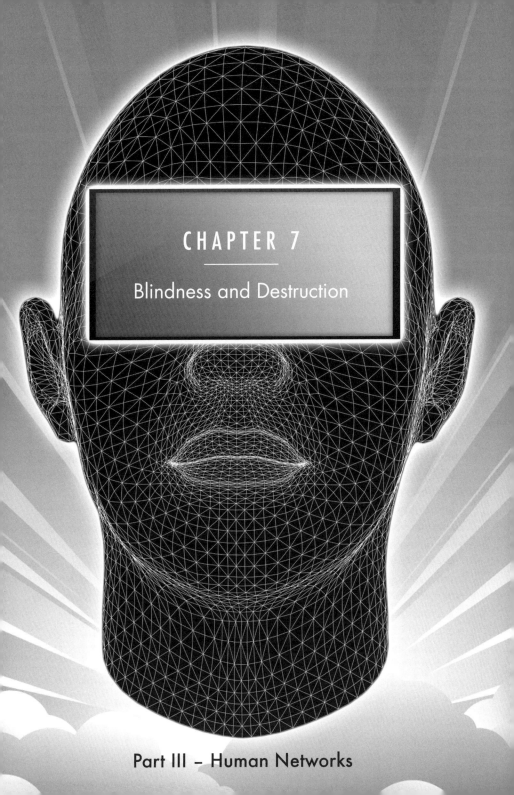

CHAPTER 7

Blindness and Destruction

Part III – Human Networks

CHAPTER 7

Blindness and Destruction

So crowds can be smart, even very smart. But they can also be self-destructive. Crowds compound errors. When, thanks to quirks in our evolution and psychological make-up, we make a common error, the crowd can compound it further. Such is the stuff that economic crises are made of; such is the stuff that leads us to war.

Many of the characteristics we evolved to suit our hunter-gatherer lifestyle can work again us. Are you a risk-taker or do you try to eliminate risk wherever possible? Imagine you take part in the game show *Deal or no Deal*. There are two boxes: in one there is £250,000 and in the other there's a penny. You are about to make your selection when someone offers you £10,000. What would you do? Your answer is a good indicator of your level of tolerance to risk.

Polarisation: North or South?

Now suppose that you are not alone, but part of a group of four people. Each of you will have a different tolerance towards risk. Common sense would suggest that such a group would take on a risk commensurate with the mean average for the group. In this case, common sense is wrong. Studies have shown that such a group tends to take a position at one of the extremes. Early studies carried out by James A. F. Stone of MIT suggested that once we join a group, we tend to take more risk. This became known as the "risky shift". However, further tests, for example, Stone's paper "Risky and cautious shifts in group decisions" indicated that a group could either take on more risks than its individuals would take when working in isolation or become more cautious. Evidence suggests that whatever the average tendency observed in a collection of individuals prior to the formation of a group, within the group we see an exaggeration. Studies by S. Moscovici, and M. Zavalloni, "The group as a polarizer of attitudes" and D. G. Myers and H. Lamm, "Group-induced Polarization of Attitudes and Behavior" used the term *group polarization* to describe this observed tendency.

Other tests (E. C. Main and T. G. Walker "Choice shifts and extreme behaviour – judicial review in the federal courts") indicated that judges working together in a group of three or more make more extreme decisions than when they work independently.

To quote Donelson R. Forsyth, "Group Dynamics": "A gathering of students who are moderately negative about a professor's teaching methods will become openly hostile after group discussion." Several examples of such polarisation exist: senior US naval officers repeatedly ignored warnings about Japanese intentions regarding Pearl Harbor[42]; Watergate was covered up and, more recently, British MPs have engaged in all sorts of creativity as regards their expense claims.[43]

It is not difficult to identify examples of groupthink. I am sure we have all fallen victim to social polarisation at some point or other in our lives.

Nonetheless, much of the academic literature on the truly important phenomenon deals with war. One of the most often cited examples concerns an attempt by the US government to oust Fidel Castro from Cuba and was advanced as an example of groupthink by Irving Janis in *Victims of groupthink; a psychological study of foreign-policy decisions and fiascos.*

Living, as we do, a few years after a war instigated to remove non-existent weapons of mass destruction from Iraq, we all have knowledge of how groupthink can go right to the very top. But the Irving example relates to a period when John F. Kennedy was US President, and the danger of nuclear war was an ever-present worry. Before Castro, Cuba was ruled by a much-hated regime. A popular uprising during 1958 resulted in the overthrow of the Batista government and in January of 1959, Fidel Castro gained power. The new leader said he was pro the US and democracy and just a few months after gaining power, he visited New York, full of charm and good intentions. He attempted to ingratiate himself with the American people,

---

[42] Irving Janis

[43] In the aftermath of the MPs' expenses scandal, popular opinion seemed to suggest MPs were grossly overpaid. Had popular opinion been given its wishes, we would have seen the political system rewind 200 years or so, with only those of a privileged background being able to afford life as an MP.

eating hamburgers and hot dogs, affirming his hatred for communism and his desire for Cuban democracy. Who knows, did Castro really believe these things or was he simply trying to cosy up to the superpower on his doorstep? Whatever the reality, he failed. President "Ike" Eisenhower was neither interested nor impressed. A rejected Castro returned home and chose instead to make overtures to the Soviets. Hell hath no fury like Castro scorned.

JFK watched the developments in Cuba with alarm. The lynchpin to his presidential campaign was the promise to halt the spread of Communism; a popular cause, it may have won him the presidency. Once in the White House he drew up plans for the removal of Castro. The CIA devised a strategy to launch a covert mission to remove the Cuban leader from power by landing highly trained troops onto a strip of Cuban land called the Bay of Pigs, from which point they were expected to draw popular support. Kennedy recruited the very best men to orchestrate the manoeuvre. So meticulous was the planning that it seemed certain to succeed. How irritating it must have been when the Institute of International Social Research produced a report warning that such an uprising would not prove popular with Cuban people. Still the IISR was clearly wrong. The group of people who hatched the plan had far too much collective wisdom for it to fail.

Yet fail it did. In fact the US government eventually had to send food and supplies to Cuba in exchange for handing back the surviving members of its force. Kennedy later asked "How could I have been so stupid?" Soon after, the Cuban Missile Crisis threatened to drag the entire world into a nuclear war; all because of an error caused initially by inaccurate groupthink.

It is not difficult to find other examples of UK and US foreign policy mistakes that had calamitous consequences. In fact, so extraordinarily inept are some of these errors that many conclude there must be some kind of conspiracy. A mysterious group of individuals, following an agenda hidden from the public, have been busy pulling strings, orchestrating a catalogue of apparent policy mistakes.

There is no conspiracy. Instead, all we have seen is evidence of how a thinking group can be extraordinarily stupid. Or, perhaps, the group can be so blind to the truth that they engage in an orgy of self-justification leading to behaviour that in hindsight seems entirely masochistic.

Such examples of groupthink are not restricted to the modern era. It is valid to suggest that the population of Ancient Athens came to a group decision which sent that state inexorably towards an unwinnable war against Sparta. If one examines Ancient Athens with certain distorted vision, ignoring the fact that the city's economy relied on slaves and that women were treated only marginally better, then you could say Athens was the most democratic city of all time. Critics of democracy cite Athens and the unreasonable behaviour that grew out of mob rule. The story of Athenian democracy proves that when a state is subject to mob rule, blind masochism often results. However, and equally true, Ancient Athens generated such creativity and cultural enlightenment that it changed the course of Western civilisation.

That's the funny thing about groupthink and crowds cooperating. They can get things horrendously wrong, but on other occasions gloriously right.

More Fool Us

Consider a scenario in which you win a ticket for a concert in a lottery. Someone offers to buy it. What do you want for it? The would-be purchaser took part in the lottery, but didn't win. Would they be willing to buy the ticket at a price you would be satisfied with? Assume that all things are equal: no hidden agenda, equal amounts of money, no romantic interest and a similar passion for the band. You might believe that the price you would charge for the ticket would be roughly the same as the price the other person would be willing to pay. This is not so. Dan Ariely, in his book *Predictably Irrational*, explored precisely this scenario among students at his university. Those who won the tickets wanted a much higher price to sell them than the students who didn't win were willing to pay. The students who won talked about how much they loved the band and how it was their dream to see them. The students who lost claimed they didn't actually like the band that much.

This is called the "endowment effect". (See Kahneman, D., J. L. Knetsch and R. H. Thaler, 1990 and 1991) Studies have repeatedly shown that we tend to put a much higher value on what we own than on what we don't. The field of psychology and behavioural economics are full of examples: we are a lot less rational that we think we are. Here are two more examples.

Firstly, consider this somewhat worrying example. Our bias and our failure to intuitively grasp mathematics can produce tragic consequences. Someone invents a test to check for breast cancer. They claim a nine in ten chance the test is accurate. What does that mean exactly? This example was given by Mlodinow: assume that one in a hundred women aged around forty develop breast cancer. Also, assume that the test never fails to identify cancer when it is in fact present. If the test is 90 per cent accurate, it means that one woman in ten will be wrongly identified as having the disease: that is to say the test will yield a "false positive" result. If one woman in one hundred has cancer and is accurately diagnosed, then ten per cent of the remaining ninety-nine will be falsely diagnosed. That's one accurate diagnosis out of 10.9 positive results. Apparently, this is a nuance of probability that doctors often do not grasp.

The key factor here is conditional probability.

Finally, there's our tendency to be influenced by preconceived notions. Take, as an example, Coca-Cola and Pepsi. You may recall the Pepsi Challenge.[44] This test seems to show that when blindfolded, people often prefer the taste of Pepsi. But, when the blindfold is removed, they prefer the taste of Coke, or so they say. Are these people lying to us? Are they examples of unmasked masochists? Tests carried out using MRI produced results showing that the pleasure centres of the brain lit up more when drinking Pepsi while wearing a blindfold, and more while drinking Coke when not wearing one.[45] In other words, people's enjoyment of refreshment really did depend on whether they knew what they were drinking.

The same principle applies to wine. Even the experts seem to get less satisfaction from a prestigious wine when a different label, synonymous with a cheaper one, is stuck on the bottle. (See Kahneman and Miller 1986.)

So what do all of our foibles have to do with crowd behaviour? Firstly, if we are aware of our fallibility, we may be more willing to comply with the crowd; surely, we think, if everyone believes a given thing to be right, then it must be. Secondly, some of these traits, such as our tendency to place a higher value on what we already have, may help loyalty to the group.

---

[44] The Pepsi Challenge was instigated by John Scully, who later left Pepsi to head Apple, famously firing Steve Jobs, only to see the computer company lose market share and eventually losing his job. Only after Jobs returned to the fold, did Apple begin its remarkable recovery.

[45] McClure, Li, Tomlin, Cypert, Montague and Montague

We value our group; we think our hunting party is best; we are more loyal to our tribe, our community, our group. Thirdly, crowd behaviour can lead to errors when the nodes that make up the network make a common mistake. Imagine you are a member of the audience on the programme *Who wants to be a millionaire?* The question is asked: Who was the last man to be proclaimed King of England before William the Conqueror? Was it:

A: Edgar the Atheling
B: Harold Godwinson
C: Edward the Confessor
D: Harold Harefoot

I assume most would say Harold Godwinson, others may think it is Harold Harefoot. Few would select the correct answer: Edgar the Atheling. That's the problem with crowds. We can be misled. If we all suffer from the same failings, then many members of a group may make the same errors, independently of each other. Then, when the group compares its conclusions and finds common agreement, the initial error gets compounded; individuals within the group become convinced they are right.

Let's All Disagree

Changing someone's mind is difficult: this is a well-accepted truism. Perhaps the problem is that in order to change our views, we quite literally have to rewire our brain. The nodes and connections which form the hub representing that view must be unlinked and reformed. The hippocampus is the key: the part of the brain associated with learning. Researchers have managed to observe the hippocampus in rats, and have actually seen evidence of new neural connections being formed as the rat learns.

Given how hard it is to reform the connections in one's own mind which form our views, consider how much harder it must be to exert change over the networks within multiple minds, not to mention the network that is formed between them. If it is hard to change the views of an individual, it is even harder to go against the crowd. Imagine you are handed two pieces of paper; on one sheet there is a straight line and on the other there are three lines of varying lengths. One looks roughly the same length as the line on the first sheet. You are asked which one of the three lines matches the original. It's easy enough to get the answer right. However, consider that you are among a group of people, each performing the same test. One by one each person calls out which line they think matches. Each person selects a different line to the one you would have chosen.

Then it's your turn. What do you do?

This was the basis of a classic study carried out by Solomon Asch. But the subject in the Asch experiment had been fooled and all but one of the people in each test group were actors who deliberately called out the wrong answer. No less than 74 per cent of subjects who took part in the experiment complied with the rest of the group, even when the group was obviously wrong on at least one occasion. A total of 34 per cent of all tests resulted in the subject changing their mind, complying with the group, and giving the wrong answer.

The Turkish psychologist, Sherif, came up with a brilliant and eerie test. He set the subjects of his experiment in a dark room and shone a single small spot of light onto a screen. After a period of time under these conditions, the light appears to move; a classic optical illusion, known as the autokinetic effect. Sherif divided his subjects into groups of three. Each person had to call out how much he or she thought the light had moved. The experiment was repeated numerous times with the same group and, over time, they converged: the estimates of the movement became more and more alike.

The Asch experiment has been repeated across the world and, although the evidence isn't clear-cut, studies[46] suggest that individuals from countries that are seen to have a more collective culture, for example Japan, Fiji and China, tend to conform more than those from more individualistic Western countries. The China example is especially interesting. It has long been suggested that Western culture, which traces its roots back to Ancient Greece (small communities isolated by the mountainous terrain) are less cooperative than the Chinese, with their emphasis on growing rice (which benefits a more cooperative form of agriculture). So, if the studies are right, then the Chinese are more likely to conform than are Westerners; the argument that groupthink is a product of a desire to conform, and that groupthink is a prime cause of financial bubbles leads to the conclusion that China is more prone to bubbles than the West.

---

[46] Bond and Smith 1996

I'm Special. Don't Change Me

Specialisation can yield outstanding benefits. However, once a network is wired in such a way that we become ultimately specialised, embracing a new opportunity becomes difficult. Within the job market this problem is clearly illustrated. One who has worked in a specific field for many years is an expert; if a new technology or technique emerges and their skill set becomes redundant, they are superfluous. People over 50, when made redundant, often find that they have to retrain, jettison years of experience, accept substantial pay reductions and, in effect, "begin again".

This is a very difficult thing to do.

Furthermore, the network can make it nigh-on impossible to introduce new, superior ideas through its propensity to adhere to that which has already become well established. Through "unfettered cooperation", where all of the nodes in the network are aligned, change can appear almost impossible. The QWERTY keyboard is a perfect example.

The original typewriter was built around a set of mechanical arms, all designed to strike the same "target". However, this mechanism was prone to jamming, particularly at high typing speeds. As a work-around, the QWERTY layout was adopted: this reduced jamming by limiting the number of adjacent keys pressed in series, and also regulated the speed of the typist. Since then, the mechanism of the typewriter has become obsolete and is now no longer used, but the QWERTY layout has persisted throughout. Even though it is counter-intuitive, even though it limits typing speed, the network has become proficient in using it. Despite the fact that a number of alternative designs have been proposed, all of which would deliver superior results, the change would be too much for most of us to bear. Individual enthusiasts may well adopt improved designs; the network is unlikely to.

Other examples abound. Automobile manufacturers would be right to be irritated by the fact that some nations drive on the left and others on the right; whilst inefficient in terms of production, this will never be changed. When the "automobile driving network" was younger (and less numerous) than it is today, Sweden, on 2 September 1967 switched their motorists from driving on the right-hand side to the left. But, even then, for a country with a relatively small road network, the operation was huge. It is by no means certain that today it would be possible, or sensible, to ask the British or the Indians to change their convention of driving on the left.

Our system for telling the time is inefficient. Would it not be easier if we had a decimal time system with 100 hours to the day and 100 minutes to the hour? In fact, the 24-hour clock dates back to the Babylonians. This is proof enough of the difficulty presented in changing non-optimal systems; our system for measuring time has persisted for millennia.

The network for fuelling vehicles has developed around the internal combustion engine, using petrol and diesel as the two forms of energy. In the longer term, electric cars may become the preferred alternative: to change the network such that the petrol pump becomes a recharge point will be a complex task. The list goes on. If only we had listened to Isambard Kingdom Brunel and upgraded our railway network, we would have a gauge of 7ft and a quarter of an inch (1.435 metres); now we are stuck with a gauge of 4ft 8 and a half inches (2.140 metres).

Change is hard to implement

A part of the problem is that in order to incorporate change, there is often a need to first move backwards: the network is not good for allowing this; the network does not have sufficient vision. And so, it crushes change. When, during the dark days of the economic crisis, the mighty General Motors was on its knees, one school of thought said: "Let it go bust. Let capitalism do its work." The vacuum that will then be left will be filled by more efficient companies. Remarkably, the motor industry itself, made up of GM's competitors, did not want the company to go bust. If it failed, so would many of its suppliers: companies that provided parts to the entire industry. In short, the automobile industry network was configured in such a way that GM had become a vital hub, feeding nodes that are vital for the survival of competing companies. In short GM, was too big too to fail.

Clearly, it is the same with banks.

The point that many overlook when they consider the question of banks, and whether they are too big to fail, is that the economic network is structured such that change to these vital hubs is incredibly hard to implement. The banking system has become resistant to change and, as will be demonstrated later, resistant to innovation.

So how do we force change in a network as complex as the economy? This, perhaps, is the most relevant question of them all.

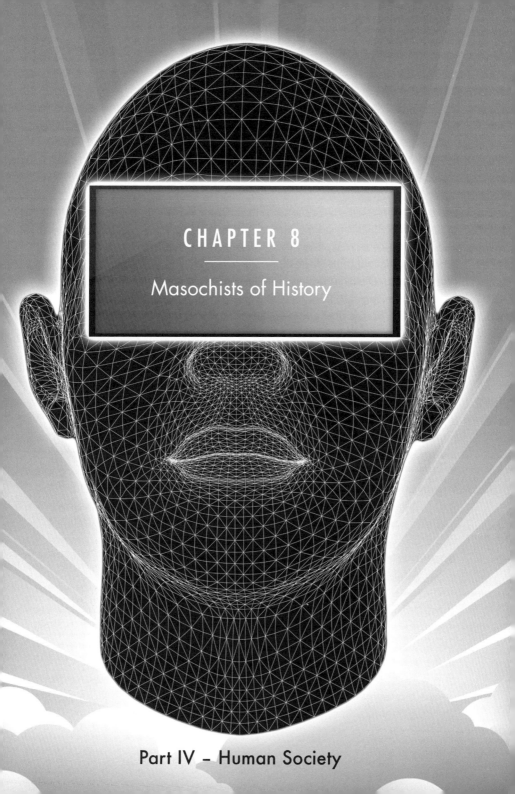

CHAPTER 8

Masochists of History

Part IV – Human Society

CHAPTER 8

Masochists of History

History is littered with examples of the blindness of the network and how we unwittingly stumble forward into disaster.

The network has no consciousness; the human beings that form an economy, a city or a civilisation are collectively unaware. Yet it is easy to be fooled into thinking otherwise. The emergent properties that can be displayed by a network can create the illusion of control: remember how the ants' nest isn't really managed by the queen? In human society, it is tempting to conclude there is a conspiracy; that an omnipotent and clandestine group exists; that they pull the strings and engineer the outcome in order to line their pockets. However, the network does not require such a conspiracy to produce the results we observe.

Some Background on Bubbles

It is not hard to think of examples of when crowds or groups can get it horrendously wrong. In economics, there have been bubbles for as long as history can recall. In these enlightened, post credit-crunch times we now live in, many people have heard of the Tulip, South Sea and Mississippi Bubbles. It is amazing, however, that during the build up to the crisis of 2008, when the mother of all credit bubbles was being formed, how few people had heard of these episodes in economic history. By 2007, even the memory of the dotcom crash was dimming in peoples' minds; at the same time a staggering number of people were saying "... of course I always knew the dotcom bubble couldn't last".

These days, the words "this time it is different", meant as an ironic statement, ring warning bells so loud that not even the deafest of ears could miss them. Other bubbles include railway mania in Britain during the 19th century and in the US some time later. Some believe China is in the midst of the formation of a bubble: that she is too reliant on exports and investment-led growth. Supporters say we are confusing Western cultural values with those of China. They say that this time, in China, it really is different. Other research, previously mentioned, indicates that Chinese cultural values make her even more prone to bubbles.

Others believe we are in the midst of a sovereign debt bubble, one that will eventually burst and dwarf the 2008 banking crisis in terms of its scale and impact. But, at least, there is a broad agreement that there is a potential sovereign debt crisis in the making, even if we are yet to find the solution. For me, a pure bubble can only be said to be formed when very few people are aware of it.

Such a bubble occurs when dissenters are few and far between: groupthink rules the network. In such circumstances individual intelligence seems to be largely irrelevant. Sir Isaac Newton himself seemed unable to calculate what in hindsight one might call the "bleeding obvious". Crowds can engage in self-reinforcing behaviour: the trajectory of their madness is directly proportional to the fortunes they think can be secured. Alas, this observation did not form any part of Newton's theories: he lost huge sums as a result of the South Sea bubble. "I can calculate the motion of heavenly bodies, but not the madness of people," said the man who described gravity, but failed to spot that what goes up in finance comes back down again.

Crowds, groupthink, collective insanity and the formation of bubbles are not exclusive to the economy. Sometimes, bubbles can be centuries in their formation. Their bursting can be swift and dramatic, however.

According to Lester R. Brown in his book *World on the Edge: How to Prevent Environmental and Economic Collapse*, Ancient Sumer caused its own downfall. Sumer's bubble was caused by salt. The world's first society to enjoy organisation on a mass scale had developed an irrigation system which led to the accumulation of salt in the soil. This eventually led to a reduction in agricultural output, forcing yet more intensive irrigation, which led to further increases in soil salinity. Look today upon the land on which were built the world's first cities, and you see deserts. In was a similar story for the Mayans, where deforestation replaced salt. In both cases the group seemed unable to spot the error in their thinking.

One example of groupthink is a story so frightening in its implications it should perhaps carry a warning: "could cause extreme distress". The story relates to the sad fate of the once rich society that dwelled on Easter Island.

The date is 5 April 1722. The Dutch explorer Jacob Roggeveen is a puzzled man. After sailing the vast expanse of the Pacific Ocean, he had finally found land: an island, miles and miles from anywhere. It was an island inhabited, or so he reckoned, by between 2000 and 3000 people. His confusion was this: while the people used canoes, cunningly designed with the limited resources available to them: they were simply not seaworthy enough to travel very far at all, let alone the two-and-a-half week journey required to reach the nearest island. Other visitors to the island puzzled over something else. How had they managed to erect such extraordinary statues? And why was it that nearly every statue was on its side, as if it has been deliberately toppled?

There have been many theories. Perhaps the most famous was advanced by Erich Von Daniken, who offered the idea that the only possible explanation is that the islanders were visited by men from outer space. His theory was somewhat undermined when the islanders made a statue in front of watching anthropologists.

The most likely explanation, however, is far more worrisome. It seems that Easter Island was once a wealthy place, with a population possibly as high as 30,000. The villagers practised a form of religion which involved the erection of statues, not dissimilar to religions seen on other Polynesian islands from which the inhabitants had probably originated. However, statues on this particular island were especially impressive and stood on equally grand platforms. It appears a kind of arms race had broken out, with the various communities on Easter Island trying to outdo each other with greater and more impressive monuments to their engineering excellence and religious fervour.

Most notably, the quarries where the stones used to erect these statues were situated in a somewhat inaccessible part of the island. Jared Diamond suggests in his book *Collapse* that they built massive ladder-like structures to transport the stones. So it continued, until there were no longer any trees from which to cut wood. To feed their appetite, it appears that the people of Easter Island robbed the land of its trees, and with that much of its wildlife. In a reaction against the religion that had brought such devastation, the people toppled the statues and, no doubt, were less than generous to the religious leaders who had advocated such destruction. A clever and creative people had sown their own destruction over the course of a few hundred years.

What puzzles Diamond, and I guess just about everyone else who reads this account, is "How could they have been so blind to their own folly?". "What did the Easter Islander who cut down the last palm tree say while he was doing it?"asks Diamond. "Like modern loggers did he shout: 'Jobs, not trees?' Or: 'Technology will solve our problems. Never fear, we will find a substitute for wood.'"

It may seem harsh to tar the IMF with the same brush as that we used to paint the story of Easter Island. The fact is, by its own admission, the IMF was a victim of groupthink during the build-up to the banking crisis; one assumes that the credit ratings agencies were equally so. For bankers, the story is different. They knew that the activities they were engaging in would eventually overheat, although it would be fair to suggest they continued in the hope that they would be able to maximise profits and cash out before disaster struck. Bankers behaved the way they did partly because of a perverse system of risk-agnostic rewards: handsome and immediate payments when things are going well; neither consequence nor punishment should their actions cause things to go badly. However, regulators, economists and politicians were all equally guilty of inaccurate groupthink. So were most of us. The debt boom that provided the foundations for the banking crisis of 2008–09 had its roots in a kind of pan-Western groupthink.

The Tyranny of the Baby Boomers

There is an excellent example of blind masochism that has been proving most pervasive of late amongst a group of like-thinking individuals: the baby boomers. Of course, I am being a little unkind. This group, and I count amongst their number, don't all hold the same views. But an element of groupthink permeates this entire generation. In Britain the baby boomers are generally defined as those people born between 1945 and the mid 1960s. In 1962, when the Beatles had their first hit, the oldest of the baby boomers were in their late teens. Some were still to be born.

Between the wars it had been quite different. The First World War had a devastating effect on a generation. Roughly 16 million deaths occurred as a result of the Great War and over 21 million were wounded. For the UK, there were just shy of one million deaths, or just over 2 per cent of the population. There were around 1.6 million wounded. This had a pulverising effect on society. The next generation were those born too late to fight in the

First World War. Many spent their formative years fighting in the Second World War.

For baby boomers it was different. The sheer scale of their numbers, and the fact that in Britain there was no fight, left them in a dominant position. It was the 1960s. "You say you want a revolution? Well, you know, we all want to change the world. You tell me that it's evolution ..." concluded John Lennon, using the word evolution in its literal sense, but almost certainly not as he meant it. The Goons were superseded by Monty Python. Humour, music, fashion and attitudes to sex all changed. A new generation, born into an age of optimism in a time of peace, but living in fear because the prospect of nuclear war was ever-present, changed society.

Their parents must have been aghast.

But, the baby boomer generation, thanks to the proportion of the population it represents, is unique in history. The extent of its influence is without precedent. When they were teenagers, the baby boomers dominated popular culture and dictated fashion to the elders. Today, they still hold sway; now their influence is over those who are younger than they are.

A crisis is in the making. What will happen when the baby boomers have all retired? In Japan, the demographic time bomb went off two decades ago: the Land of the Rising Sun has suffered twenty years of perpetual economic sunset. Japan's problem of the nineties and noughties will be the challenge of the West in the second half of this decade, the next, and indeed beyond. As McKinsey forecast, by 2056, US healthcare costs will be 100 per cent of GDP. In mainland Europe the ageing of the population is even more urgent. As the baby boomers age, they become less flexible, less willing to listen to new ideas, less willing to change. We all do this as we age. But, the baby boomers will never vote for a political party that tells them an uncomfortable truth; and democracies do what the majority requires.

The generation that changed the world has become resistant to change. The generation that gave us revolution has wrapped society in a straightjacket of intolerant tolerance. They say we have become more tolerant and yet it seems unlikely Monty Python's Life of Brian could be made today. Groupthink has claimed its victims. Although he was technically one of them Jonathan Ross, along with Russell Brand, is a victim of the tyranny of the baby boomers. A generation has turned from radicals to tyrants. A cluster within our network, rotten with groupthink, has come to a state of dominance. The consequences may not be entirely desirable. Take, as an example, one of the baby boomers' favourite topics: the property ladder.

The Property Ladder

It began during the Summer of Love in 1967; an affair that has ultimately created an unholy economic mess. Supposing you had bought a house that year, signing up to a mortgage that consumed half of your net earnings. Ouch. However, if you had maintained payments, and had your salary grown in line with economic expansion, fifteen years later your mortgage would have dwindled. By 1982, it would have cost you a mere eight per cent of your income.

Looking back in hindsight, one might say "If only. If only I had taken out a bigger mortgage; if only I had borrowed more." Of course, you can't take out a mortgage that costs more than 100 per cent of your net income; that would be impossible. Or is it? Supposing you took out a mortgage for more than you needed and spent the balance on repayments. With good timing, and after allowing for the erosion of your debt through inflation, you would be on to a winner. It would be little more than alchemy of course; the strategy has obvious pitfalls. However, such a model seems to describe the British property market. Perhaps only subconsciously, British groupthink adopted a model that enabled the creation of wealth out of a combination of leverage and inflation. Gradually, the idea that leverage is good took hold. Debt didn't matter, as its true value was eroded by inflation and in any case property prices continually rose, so higher debt was the price one paid for more wealth.

It is not clear when the metaphor "property ladder" crept into popular parlance. The first time I heard it used was in the mid-1980s; my suspicions are that the expression was a child of those times.

House prices have risen for a number of reasons. In 1967, houses were cheap. The Great Depression of the 1920s and the Second World War had devastated the value of property. By 1967 the price-to-earnings ratio represented by the average home was still low. Furthermore, back then, the government subsidised mortgages through a tax relief known as MIRAS.

Finally, interest rates were very, very low. At the time of writing, the UK's interest rates as established by the Bank of England stand at a half per cent. Most economists will tell you that since the Bank's establishment in 1694, rates have never been lower.

That's not quite true.

Earlier in the book, I investigated how the human brain is not particularly good at dealing with maths, particularly probability. Another foible we suffer from is the illusion of money. We don't intuitively understand the concept of inflation. On an academic level we might; on a visceral one, we don't. This illusion has led to the mistaken belief that interest rates in April 2011 are at an all-time low. In 1975, inflation was 24.2 per cent; the bank rate was 11 per cent. Real interest rates were, therefore, negative 13 per cent. In the 1960s and 1970s, inflation came to the aid of mortgage holders, rapidly eroding the real value of their debt. Put simply, inflation paid for the mortgages of an entire generation. House prices kept rising; the real cost of mortgages kept falling. We fell for the problem of induction. Money illusion and the confirmation bias set in, and were reinforced by groupthink. "House prices always rise," they said. Even though, for a while in the 1970s, the property prices fell, it was merely a fall in price relative to inflation. Why was this not widely reported? Money illusion.

As ever, there are a huge number of reasons offered to justify the perpetual rise in house prices. The UK is an island; land is in short supply. That's true, but Japan is made up of islands as well, and their house prices have been falling for 20 years. The Dutch don't have much land and yet have never experienced a similar property boom. Is there a shortage of homes? Again, not true. Over six million households in the UK have more than one spare bedroom.[47]

---

[47] The following is taken by *Bubbles and Wisdom* from Michael Baxter and Kenn Herskind. "Capital Economics released a report in May 2008 looking at the argument that there was an under-supply of housing. It defined under-occupancy in this way. It assumed: a separate bedroom for each married or cohabiting couple, for any person aged 21 or over, or for each pair of adolescents aged 10–20 years of the same sex (a pair of adolescents aged 10–20 years of the opposite sex are assumed to have individual bedrooms), and for each pair of children under 10 years. A home is deemed to be under-occupied when there are two or more bedrooms above the bedroom standard. Apparently, according to the Survey of English Housing, no less than 47 per cent of existing owner-occupier dwellings – that's 6.8 million homes – are under-occupied. Tellingly, only 18 per cent of private rented properties are under-occupied."

Why so much spare space? Surely it is partly because householders see property as an investment. Given the assumptions detailed above, it is worth remaining in a property larger than required: the additional expense is part of the retirement nest egg.

In the post credit-crunch era, we look back at the madness of the credit boom as a function of greed; we borrowed more than we could afford. Now, we must all live within our means. However, examining the debt-fuelled craze of the 1990s and 2000s through the prism of rising house prices, such leverage appears logical. It would have worked in 1967, after all. The dotcom crash made matters worse. The lesson of the dotcom bubble was that stocks were not safe. Investors migrated from clicks, to clicks and mortar, to bricks and mortar. It was a hard-learnt lesson, except the lesson was wrong. At least the dotcom boom helped advance the Internet.

Rising house prices don't promote wealth. They distribute wealth.[48] The stock market boom of the 1990s led to overconfidence regarding pensions amongst companies, the government as well as households. Corporate entities paid less into their pension schemes; Gordon Brown removed tax credits from pension contributions: we became confident that our retirement would be funded from the growth in our assets.

The stock market crash of 2000 panicked people.[49] All of a sudden, the realisation crept in that our retirement would not be quite so trivial to fund. As a result, we fled to property. Unfortunately, just because house prices are rising, it does not necessarily mean we are able to produce more goods and services. Any resulting rise in wealth is an illusion.

---

[48] Adam Smith said in his book *The Wealth of Nations*, published in 1776: A dwelling-house, as such, contributes nothing to the revenue of its inhabitant; and though it is, no doubt, extremely useful to him, it is as his clothes and household furniture are useful to him, which, however, makes a part of his expense, and not of his revenue. If it is to be let to a tenant for rent, as the house itself can produce nothing, the tenant must always pay the rent out of some other revenue which he derives either from labour, or stock, or land. Though a house, therefore, may yield a revenue to its proprietor, and thereby serve in the function of a capital to him, it cannot yield any to the public, nor serve in the function of a capital to it, and the revenue of the whole body of the people can never be in the smallest degree increased by it."

[49] As of 28 May, 2011, the FTSE 100 still languishes below the all time high set on 30 January 1999 of 6930.

What will happen when the baby boomers retire and release wealth from their homes to fund their retirement? The answer is clear: people will demand more than can be produced. Unless there is dramatic growth in immigration, a phenomenon that British groupthink is diametrically opposed to, demand will exceed supply, bringing inflation; interest rates will rise in the first instance to combat inflation and, in the second, to reflect the fact that there are less savings. As soon as interest rates return to normal levels, house prices in the UK will face an insurmountable challenge. At that point, property value will crash; furthermore, it will remain permanently low.

The government should have tightened rules on owning a second home, removed the way buy-to-let investors can offset interest against tax, and relaxed planning regulations. But such measures would have been seen as an attack on the baby boomers, and their tyranny would never have allowed it. The consequences for the economy and the baby boomers in particular will be dire. The network represented by the UK's homebuyers, so fooled by money illusion, the law of small numbers and the problem of induction, suffering from confirmation bias and blinded by groupthink, will suffer a substantial amount of self-inflicted pain.[50]

The Illusion of Equities

It was not only house prices that seduced us. The City and financial advisors, those allegedly "in the know", were also taken in, but by a different kind of asset.

In the late 1990s, if you had sought investment advice, it is likely you would have been told that in the long run equities always increase in value. The worst consequence of either bad luck or bad timing would be short-term losses. Advisors said that by taking a long-term view, purchasing equities and reinvesting dividends, a good deal of money could be made. Strangely unmentioned would have been the fact that equities had outperformed the economy for decades. How is that possible? If the economy grows at 2.5 per cent a year, how can equities appreciate at a consistently higher rate?

There are few explanations. One is that a higher percentage of companies were floated on the stock market; the steady rise in the value of equities can be attributed to a larger proportion of the economy as a whole being publicly traded. There's truth in that explanation but, on its own, it is insufficient. It is equally true that globalisation played a large part with many companies listed in London not trading that actively in the UK; but this explanation is not sufficient to explain the increases: how can increases in equity valuations exceed global GDP growth? And the third factor that played a part in driving up equity values? Optimism.[50]

Over time the "hope value" of companies steadily rose. Academics spoke of the rise in "risk premia" as, over decades, investors steadily took on more risk when investing into companies. By the late 1990s, an investor's favourite anecdote was to recall how quickly shares recovered from the 1987 crash, and how a diversified portfolio had reclaimed its previous value so quickly. Such was the power of equity investment; so convincing the story sold by the industry.

Nonetheless, investors were victims of the biases and glue that permeate groupthink. When a company is valued, its share price should reflect future dividends, discounted by a rate of interest, to give a net current value. If equities steadily rise, this implies that previous valuations underestimated future income. For equities to continually rise, investors must always underestimate long-term potential. Yet, from the mid-1970s onwards, economic growth was a disappointment. The golden years of growth were from the end of the war to the early part of that decade. From there on in, performance was below expectation.

So, if the economy performed worse than expected, how is it possible for investors to have continually underestimated the long-term potential of the firms in which they purchased stock? For most of the second half of the last century, dividends on equities were lower than yields on bonds. The euphoria of that time confirmed the belief: "That's the way it's supposed to be." We too easily forget that in the first half of the 20th Century, yield on bonds was lower than dividends on equities. A reversion to the older pattern is quite possible, and if this happens, equities will fall sharply, making it even harder to fund the retirement of the baby boomers.

For decades, investors blindly held to the doctrine that equities always rise in the long-term. For many years their belief became self-fulfilling. Their

---

[50] Of course, we could meet demand via imports, but this brings it own dangers. In any case, the entire planet cannot solve the problem of ageing with increased imports.

optimism caused the very thing they expected to happen; this reinforced their optimism. The success enjoyed by equities lulled us all into a false sense of security: a prosperous retirement was assured. Savings rates fell; who needs big savings when equities keep rising?

Fooled, In Tandem

It was the interplay between the false belief both in equities and house prices that created a "buy now, pay later" culture, one of low savings and inadequate provisions for retirement. Such an unfortunate mix of blind, misplaced faith had another more serious consequence. The real driver of economic growth is innovation. Innovation comes from dynamism. The success of the money-for-nothing generation, typically the baby boomers, gradually pulled would-be entrepreneurs away from enterprises that could create real wealth into rent-seeking. Rent-seeking is fine when you are retired. In fact, retirement can only be funded by living off other people's work. We get fooled by the metaphor called "money" into thinking otherwise.

"I worked hard all my life and saved my money: now I can fund my retirement." This is only true to an extent. Even if we have diligently saved all of our lives, in retirement we are still reliant on others. You cannot eat money, drink it or live in it. Saved money is irrelevant unless there are a sufficient number of people out there creating goods and services. Should the money we spend through digging into savings be greater than the monetary value of goods and services in the economy, inflation sets in, discounting the value of our savings.

There is nothing that can be done about the fact that when we are older it may no longer be viable for us to work. So, during our working years, the key is not to save but to find ways for the generation that succeeds us to produce and provide. In other words, it is not so much savings that count, but investment: and the right kind of investment at that. Consider this argument from the perspective of the self-sufficient community of hunter-gatherers. In such a community, saving for the long term is pointless. What is useful is discovery: how to make knives sharper, how to improve on hunting tactics, the efficiency of gathering and the preservation of food. The entire economic network is analogous to such a community. Those of working age who are rent-seeking as opposed to wealth-creating are counterproductive.

The network, throughout much of the working lives of the baby boomers, has conspired to throttle real wealth creation.

This masochism is made complete: had the baby boomers promoted true wealth creation via innovation, equities could indeed have risen year on year in a sustainable way.

Trickle Down

The economic network is blind in more than one way. It has managed to pull off the rare trick of creating alignment in the hubs and nodes so that the network, simultaneously, is unfair and inefficient. Seduced by the metaphor that Darwinian evolution is best described as "survival of the fittest," we all accept that life is unjust: that the "dog eat dog" notion of evolution is the way we progress.

Consider the idea that the economy needs the super-rich because their wealth trickles down to benefit everyone else. The argument suggests that the rewards enjoyed by the super-rich are incentives, encouraging them to go forth and create more wealth for the benefit of the general public. We should be grateful for the super-rich. Does it matter if some people enjoy incomes in excess of one million pounds a year off the back of their hard work and innovation? Surely their success is a benefit to society. Such is the nature of the trickle-down philosophy. We're all better off thanks to the super-rich; don't tax them or reduce their income, or we punish ourselves. Those wishing to reduce the disparity of wealth distribution are practising the politics of envy.

The only problem with this line of reasoning is that it is wrong.

This is not to say that there should not be high rewards for big risks. It is not to say that working hard, being clever, achieving high standards and receiving commensurate benefits is wrong. This is essential for wealth creation. However, there is always an unpleasant aroma whenever a mild belief becomes extreme. Over the last quarter-century, there has been a gradual shift in attitude. Trickle-down economics gained momentum. The rich got richer; we all enjoyed the benefit.

In the UK, the Labour Party, after their election defeat of 1992, accepted the new thinking; as a result, the party was reformed as New Labour and the Third Way. It was the defeat of socialism and the victory of a new philosophy, a philosophy that meant sustainable wealth creation for everyone. It was in keeping with this new thinking that Peter Mandelson made his pronouncement: "We are intensely relaxed about people getting filthy rich ... as long as they pay their taxes." And so, on the back of the reforms made by Thatcher, the New Labour government of 1997 became a card-carrying disciple of the new philosophy. The economy boomed; the UK enjoyed its longest ever run of uninterrupted economic growth. Economists and politicians congratulated each other on their new era of constant growth. The electorate, drunk on their own prosperity, egged them on.

No one dared suggest we were living a lie, but we were.

We seemed oblivious to even the most transparent lie of the lot: the belief our income was increasing. Ernst & Young produced the figures that reveal the lie. In 2008 it released data showing that monthly discretionary income for a typical household had dropped 15 per cent over the four-year period from 2003–04 to 2008 when the report was published. At the time of its report, it said that "The average household now has £772.79 to spend each month after total fixed monthly outgoings, compared with £909.84 in 2003–04." It was surely a damning indictment of the alleged economic success story.

But although households were struggling, they kept spending: thanks to leverage the spending boom continued. The apparent increase in wealth gained through rising house prices was used to fund our spending. We were told that this wasn't a problem, that consumer spending was not rising faster than GDP; talk of consumption overheating was dismissed as a myth. In truth, during the late 1990s, consumption grew at such a pace that by the beginning of the millennium the consumer should have been exhausted. Not even Usain Bolt can cover ground that fast.

Overstretched consumers and the dotcom crash should, by rights, have created recession; that they didn't can only be attributed to low interest rates and lots of spare credit. As a consequence of this, house prices soared and people felt better off than they should. What we saw in 2008–09 was the inevitable consequence of excesses of the 1990s, but delayed. Even then, despite the severity of the recent recession, the cracks were papered over. Rock-bottom interest rates have staved off disaster; we have not yet paid the price for our historical greed. Ironically, the 1980s are often referred to as the decade of greed; in truth it is the 1990s that allowed the rot to take hold.

While households became worse off during the boom, their discretionary disposable income during the worst recession to hit the UK in 80 years actually improved. Sure, unemployment rose and hit some households hard: those with work and mortgages found that the fall in interest rates meant they had more spare money, not less.

However, there is another way of looking at this: the real consequences of 1990s excess are still being hidden from us. Alas, looking forward, things will go into reverse. The Centre for Economics and Business Research (CEBR) predicts that, after falling 0.8 per cent in 2010, household disposable income, at the time of writing, is set to fall 2 per cent in 2011. If it proves right, then the contraction will be the biggest fall since the recession of 1919–1921.

And yet, as households suffer, corporates don't know what to do with their cash. What we are seeing in both the UK and US is the unfolding of a scenario in which corporates are cutting costs and wages are falling relative to inflation. However, companies are not spending. They don't know what to do with the spare cash created by their cost cutting. Given that they have few alternatives, they are using their cash holdings either to fund mergers and acquisitions, big dividend payouts or share buybacks, or simply hoarding it. There is a potential problem here. An economy needs demand. When Henry Ford paid workers at his factories $5 a day, more than double the going rate at the time, a part of his rationale was that if by doing this he could trigger wage rises across the economy, more people would be able to buy his cars.

If wages are not rising, if income is being skewed by uneven distribution, where will growth in demand come from? GDP is made up of consumption, investment, government spending and exports minus imports. The consumption element is predominantly funded by wages, dividends or debt. Across the world today, governments are cutting spending. Relying on investment to drive growth is a problem: companies will only invest if they think there is demand for the extra productivity their investment will produce.

It is fine for an economy to rely on exports, but the world can't export more than it imports. For an individual country, exports may make up GDP; for the global economy exports must equal imports. In other words, consumer demand is critical. Without growth in consumer demand, GDP growth will stutter. For demand to grow in a sustainable way, wages must rise. Not only is that not happening now, it hasn't been happening for a while. As Rebecca Wilder said on the *Angry Bear* blog: "Higher demand increases sales rates, revenues and production which grows firm profits that are translated into wage and income gains, only to drive demand further upward. It's broken right between 'grows firm profits' and 'translated into wage and income gains'."

This is a worldwide problem too. In China, wage growth has been lagging behind GDP growth for decades, although there are signs that this is changing.

What we are seeing is a growing divide in the developed world between the richest and the poorest. Even those in the middle are being left behind. Raguram G. Rajan, a former chief economist at the IMF argues in his book *Fault Lines* that the surge in house prices disguised this effect. He says: "Politicians have therefore looked for other ways to improve the lives of their voters. Since the early 1980s, the most seductive answer has been easier credit. In some ways it is the path of least resistance. So is this all deliberate? Is there a conspiracy to placate US households with the bribe of easier credit, funded by surging house prices?"

Network theory would suggest there is no need for bribes. The network is quite capable of creating its own imbalances. It needs no higher intelligence, no clandestine group pulling strings. As Rajan says, "It may well be that many of the parts played by the key actors were guided by the preferences and applause of the audience, rather than by well-thought-out intent. Put differently, politicians may have tried different messages until one resonated with voters."

Rajan says the problem is that the US education system seems to be favouring the elite. Dambisa Moyo says in her book *How the West Was Lost* that demographics and immigration are set to exasperate the problem. Focusing on the US she says that those who benefit from the elite US education system are seeing their numbers dwindle. The US does not suffer from the same demographic problems we face in Europe. Its population is set to carry on rising. But the part of the US population that is set to rise is the same part that has been traditionally squeezed out from the best of the

US education system. For that reason, Moyo reckons the US economy will stagnate rapidly during the middle years of this decade. "If nothing else changes it from its current path," she says. "It is almost certain that America will move from a fully fledged capitalist society of entrepreneurs to a socialist nation within a few decades ... the trouble is," she adds, "it won't be just any socialist welfare state ... the US is on the path to creating the venal form of welfare state (poorly developed and designed) – one born of desperation from many years of flawed economic policies and a society that rapaciously feeds on itself."

Political thinking from the time of Thatcher right up to the beginning of the credit crunch was that it did not matter if we saw the rich get richer, because much of the wealth they create trickles down and benefits everyone else. The trickle-down argument is no longer looking credible.

One of the problems you have with the creation of such a large divide between the rich and the rest is that our doctors and our dentists demand higher wages. We have to pay them more, or else they will opt for careers in the City. As a result, doctors and dentists now enjoy salaries that, in turn, are making health care unaffordable. In the UK the NHS is a ravenous monster that is never satisfied. In the US, the health care crisis in the making is far worse. There is also the issue of trust. An extreme form of distribution of wealth or uneven opportunity creates distrust. Various studies, from among others Francis Fukuyama and Robert D. Putnam, show there is a link between levels of trust and prosperity within an economy: A finding that is broadly backed up by the World Values Survey.

Then of course, there is the issue of bankers' pay. As Will Hutton says in his book, *Them and Us*, "The British are happy to accept that hard work, innovation risk and effort should be rewarded. The entrepreneurs dream, scheme and create to drive forward our economy – and our society ... But rewards today do not fall to entrepreneurs who risk everything. They go to executives and financiers who do not risk their own money." And, as Lord Turner at the FSA once said, most of what banks do is "socially useless".

Another issue here is globalisation. It is what the IMF calls "the globalisation of labour". Also of relevance is what's called the Paradox of Thrift. According to Keynes, in an economic depression, such as the 1930s, consumers tend to save more because they are worried about the future, but, as the rate of saving rises, aggregate demand across the economy falls and the depression gets even worse. Keynes advocated channelling wealth into the poorer households, because poorer families tend to save less. He suggested that in times of depression money should be taken from the rich and given to the poor. He was no socialist; far from it. He made these comments because, under certain circumstances, he saw this as the best thing for the economy.

Since the credit crunch, two new theories have emerged, building on the Paradox of Thrift.

The Paradox of Toil was suggested by Gauti Eggertsson, an economist who works at the Fed in New York. He argued that under certain circumstances, if workers start to work harder, then the result can be a rise in unemployment and falls in wages. The theory is based on certain conditions: that the economy is suffering from deflation, that there's declining output, and that interest rates are zero. Of course, such circumstances would be especially worrisome if consumers or their government are highly indebted, because falling wages would be rather bad news for those carrying debt. Another theory is the Paradox of Flexibility. This one, from Lynne Gouliquer, a sociologist, draws similar conclusions, but from a scenario in which labour market flexibility leads to falling wages.

The key point to bear in mind here is that demand drives corporate profits, and demand is determined by wages. So, if the cost of labour falls, companies make more money in the short run. However, in the long run, aggregate demand falls, leading to declining profits.

Globalisation is not a bad thing. It creates wealth and could do much to help end poverty. But the network is blind. Globalisation is creating a massive disparity between the few and the rest. This is not merely a moral problem, in the longer term, but economically inefficient. Where will the demand come from to feed global growth?

Not Just Blind, but Masochistic Too

The stories and metaphors that we love don't help. Harry, Ron and Hermione save the Muggles. Little Frodo and Sam save Middle Earth. Fiction is full of stories of heroes: of how the few save the many. This helps reinforce the view that we need to reward the few, in order to incentivise them to save us, from ourselves. History books on the Industrial Revolution talk about John Kay, James Hargreaves, James Watt, Stephenson, Brunel and the economic heroes who made Britain great. But, as was pointed out in Chapter 6, it was the workers. It was the army of engineers. Together, they made hundreds, perhaps thousands, of small innovations. These are the events that really drove the Industrial Revolution.

Will Hutton quotes the Noble Prize winner Herbert Simon to make a similar point. The Nobel winner "reckons," says Hutton, "that nobody can attribute more than 20 per cent of their earnings and originality to their own efforts; the rest builds on the collective intellectual legacy."

As previously stated, groups can be wise, and can out-think individuals. Society says that huge salaries are the best reward for hard work. This is an absurd statement. Do you really believe the millions of people on average wages don't work hard? Plenty of people work hard all their lives and barely lift their heads above the parapet of poverty. The network has fooled us. It has conspired to create a system that is unnecessarily unfair, immoral and unsustainable. Worse still, it has fooled us over and over again. Ultra-high salaries are supposed to be the reward for hard work and innovation. Nonetheless, network theory shows why this is not true.

A network automatically forms hubs. It automatically tends to throw up a distribution of hubs that follow a power law. The process known as preferential attachment shows that the rich get richer regardless of how hard they work or how clever they are. There is even a simulation of a simple economy produced on a computer which shows how the super rich develop with only slight correlation with cleverness or skill. The model, developed by Joshua Epstein and Robert Axtell, researchers at Michigan University, was covered in their book *Growing Artificial Societies: Social Science from the Bottom Up* and is called Sugarscape. In this model, sugar crops and sugar production varies across a grid. Agents, each of which needs sugar to survive and flourish, each with varying abilities and metabolism are placed at random around the grid. The simulation begins: each agent sets off in search of sugar. When it finds it, it consumes the sugar for the purpose of both survival and the creation of a reserve of wealth. Since some of these agents have superior skills to others, you would expect them to be more successful at finding sugar. To an extent, that is how it works, but only to an extent. In time, the simulation throws up a small super class of exceedingly sugar-rich agents. Then, there is a larger group of rich and successful agents, then a much bigger group of middle class agents and finally a much larger mass of poor, impoverished agents. The distribution of wealth follows a power law, but the distribution of ability does not.

So, it is not true to say that the super-rich get rich because of their ability. The uneven distribution of wealth exists because *that's how networks work*. We too easily fool ourselves into believing that our wealth is attributable to naked ability and hard work.

We think we have more control than we really do. Consider an experiment conducted among students at Yale University. For each student, a coin was tossed several times, and they were asked to guess the outcome. Researchers deliberately manipulated the results so that students got exactly half their guesses right. Then they asked questions such as, "Could you have done better with more practise?" or, "Would you have done better if you had been distracted less before making your guesses?" Amazingly, many of them (remember they were students at one of the top universities in the world) answered yes. Somehow, they felt they had some influence over the outcome. We all do it. You see gamblers conducting their ritual: if they blow on the dice, and say ten Hail Marys, and throw it, they get the result that they want. This does not influence the outcome: even without the ritual the result, on occasion, will be as they would like it to be. It's about pure chance. A business deal comes off. Was it really down to the people involved? Did they work really hard? Are they really astute? The real question is: were they lucky? Nonetheless, it is rare that people acknowledge or accept that.

It is not to say that some super-rich aren't extremely clever. It's not to say that they don't work very hard. It is equally true to say that some are neither. The argument that the super-rich are that way because they deserve it is based on a false assumption. Those who say that the super-rich are necessary to generate wealth, citing the US as an example, conveniently forget that the more egalitarian Scandinavian economies are among the most successful in the world. Indeed, if you look back over the course of economic history, it does seem to be true that those societies in which there is a less even distribution of wealth do not enjoy significant growth. Throughout the Medieval period, right up to the early 19th Century, economic growth was inconsequential. It was only after the emergence of a middle class, where "wages for the many" started to rise, that economic growth began to take off. The golden era of growth, in the post war period, was one in which society had become more egalitarian. But, so complete is the illusion created by the network, that by 2011, the view began to set in that the poor somehow deserved their plight. Ian Cowie argued in the *Daily Telegraph*, with his piece, *A tax-based alternative to the Alternative Vote*, that the unemployed should not be allowed to vote in elections. A government minister suggested that it should be possible to buy your way into university.

The network has fooled us; the network has lied to us. It has not lied because it is immoral, because it has no self-awareness. But it is amoral, it is most certainly blind, and seems to be in love with inflicting pain: upon itself.

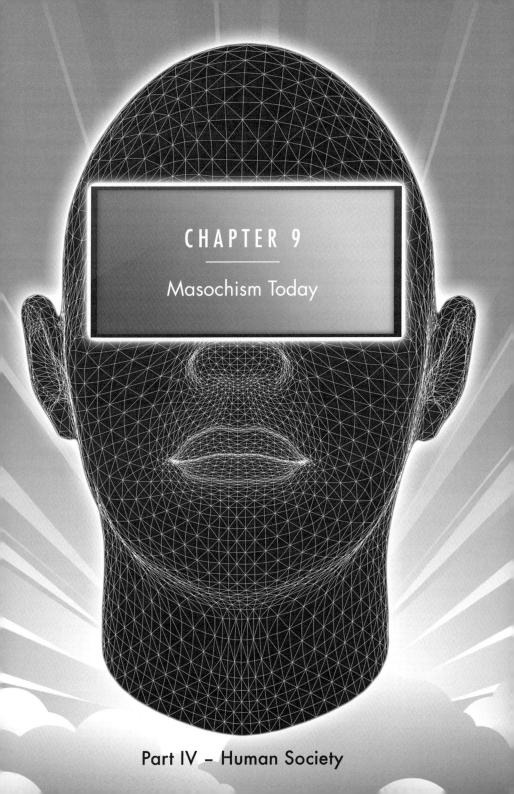

CHAPTER 9

Masochism Today

Part IV – Human Society

CHAPTER 9

Masochism Today

It all boils down to groupthink. Can we turn the power of the crowd to our advantage, let collaborative learning and understanding make us rich in mind as well as body, or will we let ourselves be dragged down by group polarisation, blindly rushing towards economic and social oblivion?

As stated previously, the challenge for the baby boomers lies not so much with how they save. It lies with what they do with their savings. If they pour their hard-earned money into property and in the process do little to advance innovation, then they have been fooled. They may think a prosperous retirement is assured; if this practice was followed by a small minority then that may be the case. But, across the network, the only way to meet the needs of this entire generation is to ensure their activities promote new and more efficient ways of producing goods and services. This is the illusion of saving. As far as the baby boomers are concerned, "it's not what they do, it's how they do it, and that's what gets results".

The solution lies with entrepreneurs; the people who can go out and create real wealth and through the alchemy of innovation turn cash into opportunity. The danger lies with banks. Both entrepreneurs and banks reflect aspects of the blindfolded masochist.

Entrepreneurs: Blindfolded Optimists

To illustrate the problem of entrepreneurs, consider Walter Raleigh's plans to set up the first English colony in what we now called the United States. Raleigh went ahead: the settlement of Roanoke Island in modern day North Carolina was formed. It failed spectacularly. No one knows why. All we know is that a few years after the colony was founded, a ship docked with new provisions, but no one was there.

The truth is the United States was built on risk taking; risk taking of such breathtaking audacity, that one would be forgiven for describing it as irrational. Then again, risk has been with us from the start, from the moment we stepped down from the trees.[51]

New businesses often go the same way. If you are an entrepreneur, failure hurts more than is commonly realised. A real entrepreneur puts his or her soul into their business. They put their credibility on the line. If their business fails, the blow to their confidence, to their reputation, to their credibility, can be fatal. If they are able to find it within themselves to try again, the next time they may be successful. If they can somehow find something good, something close to working in their failed business, they might find something to build upon. In practice, society (especially British society) so dislikes failure, it is very hard indeed for an entrepreneur to elicit the support required for a second stab. It is a terrible price so many failed entrepreneurs pay having had the courage to try to make something of a bold idea.

As Will Hutton says in *Them and Us*, "The European Flash Barometer found that around 43 per cent of people in the UK (compared with 19 per cent in the US) believe that a new business should not be created if there is a risk it may fail."

It is not quite like that in the US. Henry Ford's early business ventures ended in disaster, leaving him broke. It was similar story with Rowland Hussey Macy, who suffered a run of failed business before he finally managed to establish Macy's store. Walt Disney was something of a serial entrepreneur, but his ventures had been disasters, until he formed his Mickey Mouse company. Other famous Americans who had either suffered bankruptcy, or at the very minimum had found themselves with massive debts, include Donald Trump, Mark Twain, Francis Ford Coppola (before the first *Godfather* movie), and William C. Durant, the founder of General Motors, who filed for bankruptcy in 1936. Perhaps, most remarkably of all, Abraham Lincoln was declared bankrupt in 1833, three decades before becoming the most famous president in US history. Unfortunately, the relationship between bankruptcy and success often works the other way round, Ulysses S. Grant incurred massive debts after he was president, and Buffalo Bill lost all his money. The list of celebrities, including some of the most famous, who suffered bankruptcy after their fame had peaked is actually quite surprising.

These examples show success is not a foregone conclusion. Just as failure is a key part of Darwinian natural selection, so it is inevitable in the realm

---

[51] Be grateful there weren't any health and safety inspectors then, for we would have never taken the plunge.

of wealth creation. In some cases, the problem is regression to the mean. Bankruptcy follows success because the person concerned fell into the trap of thinking all their riches were down to their talents, and that they could do no wrong.

Attitudes to failure are crucial. In the UK, we don't tend to hear much about the failures. We hear only of the successes and we try and learn from their experiences. So, we hear about the entrepreneur who left school at 16 with a CSE in woodwork and is now worth millions, and we ask, "What good is education?" Or, we hear about two others, who left education while studying for a PhD to form a dotcom, which is now worth billions and we talk about the benefits of the network that this duo formed while at university.

The truth is that every successful entrepreneur is different. Many unsuccessful entrepreneurs share the characteristics that seem so essential for success.

There are signs that attitudes are changing for the better. TV programmes such as the *Apprentice* or *Dragons Den* have helped make entrepreneurialism sexy. The programmes in question may present a distorted view, but at least they present a view. For too long kids harboured the dream of being the next Robbie Williams or David Beckham. Even though the craving is for celebrity, a growing number wish now to be entrepreneurs.

A paper entitled "Impact of Media on Entrepreneurial Intentions and Actions", by Levie, Hart and Shamsul Karim produced encouraging results. It concluded that around half the sample of non-entrepreneurs thought more positively about entrepreneurs in general and were made more aware of a career as an entrepreneur through the media. Of those who were so positively minded, saying yes, just over half reported that television was where they came across the terms most often. Almost half of non-entrepreneurs also said they had watched television programmes in the last 12 months which showed how to start or run a business. According to research from Hiscox, no less than 40 per cent of students in London are either running their own business or are about to do so. Hull, the city that has suffered from permanent economic depression for decades, is second in its chart of would-be entrepreneurs. These are encouraging developments. Give someone who is unemployed the hope that comes with setting up a business, then the despondency that comes with being unemployed for years can metamorphose into optimism. Give a thug the chance of running a business, and the thug trades his hoodie for a suit – PowerPoint replaces the knife as the tool of his trade.

Were more people self-employed, more wealth might trickle down to permeate a higher percentage of society.

Banks: Rational Masochists

Irrational optimism drives risk takers who, from time to time, can make the greatest advances. However, the network has developed in such a way as to work against the very behaviour that benefits it. Imagine you are seeking to fund risk takers. You provide them with the funding they say they need. In return you enjoy a fixed return, roughly commensurate with the rate of interest.

Such a lending strategy makes no sense. If the business you are funding fails, your money is lost. If it succeeds, you enjoy a return proportional to the interest rate, which will never be sufficient to fund the money you lose. You respond to this by being more conservative in your lending. You may decide you can only afford to fund a business if it can make interest payments with its existing cash flow. Or, you may choose to put your money into something low risk, such as property.

Funding the more risky businesses is, therefore, left to the venture capitalists.

During the boom years of the nineties and noughties it was much harder to obtain bank funding for a small business, especially a new business, than for spending on a jolly. Indeed, if you needed funding for your business, there were advantages in lying, claiming that you were planning to spend the money on a holiday. When viewed on a case-by-case basis, such a lending strategy makes sense. The consequence is that funding flows to low risk operations, including property speculation; operations that may not create much wealth. As such, the provision of funding to business is back to front. Most funding comes in the form of bank loans, at low risk. Venture capital is relegated to the fringe. When the entire economy focuses on lending over sharing in profits, the result is an economy that is less risky at the node level; however, at the network level it is substantially more so.

That's the great irony of the banking crisis. Banks chose to supply funding for assets they saw as low risk. But, in so doing, they were not providing the lubrication the economy needed to expand. Instead, their funding turned would-be entrepreneurs into rent seekers. When an economy is dominated by rent seekers over wealth creators, a new form of risk emerges.

A bigger problem is that banks are seen as vital to the system. They are not allowed to fail. New players are crowded out; the old ones repeat their errors. In the UK, the Bank of England recently adopted the policy of quantitative easing (QE), in the hope of forcing up asset prices, particularly government bonds, making alternatives seem worthwhile. By doing so, conditions might return to normal, equities would rise, property prices would rise and lending would increase. Through QE, both the UK's central bank and the Fed in the US were risking a repeat of the errors that caused the crisis in the first place.

Leverage is seductive. If you can borrow money and see the purchased asset rise in value, your net wealth can soar. However, when a boom based on leverage unwinds as seen in 2008, the results are catastrophic. By contrast, a boom funded by investment capital and shared profits is inherently more stable. The bubble may eventually burst, but as the dotcom crash showed, the damage caused is less serious, as are the economic consequences. Behaviour which, on node level seems logical and prudent, is catastrophic for the network. When hubs get sucked into the illusion of safety, the potential for crisis worsens. An economic system whereby hubs reduce risk through squashing innovation is a characteristic of the blindfolded masochist.

The Innovator's Dilemma

Consider the disc drive industry. The classic study here was carried out by Clayton M. Christensen.

He chose the disc drive industry because it had changed so fast and had seen the emergence of a number of disruptive technologies over a short period of time. For each one, the network was re-configured: companies that had formerly dominated the industry went bust, making space for new ones. The network makes it nigh on impossible for incumbent players to change. At one point in the industry's history, the leading technology was the 8″ floppy, as used in mini-computers. The market was dominated by a handful of companies who had operated from inception of the market; they had incorporated the latest technology and were proven innovators. New entrants to the markets were largely unsuccessful.

The emergence of 5.25 inch disk drives for desktop computers changed everything. Many of the existing market leaders examined the new technology; some invested. However, they stopped short of embracing it; their customers used mini-computers and were not interested in "here today gone tomorrow" desktops. By the time the desktop market was established, with 5.25 inch drives showing signs of dominance, it was too late. The new entrants, with their specialisation in the latest technology, held all the cards. The former heavyweights lost market share; many went out of business.

This was not a one-off. Christensen was able to show that the business saw similar shifts several times. The giants of the 8 inch disk drive market should have learned from the decline of 14 inch drives for mainframes. The new kids, in the 5.25 inch market, were no wiser. When notebooks became more popular and 3.5 inch drives began to take off, they too were caught sleeping. In each case, be it 8 inch, 5.25 inch or 3.5 inch the technology was nothing special to begin with: the new players were using off-the-shelf components. Crucially, they became specialised, their network of expertise more sophisticated, more complex and more entrenched. The older companies found that their specialisation was a disadvantage: change was too hard. Changing sooner might have preserved their position of strength. In other words, Christensen showed how disruptive technology can cause established players to fail.

The innovator's dilemma is not a new idea. The Austrian economist Joseph Schumpeter developed a theory to explain precisely that: he called it Creative Destruction, famously referring to "great gales" of it.

Because large, market-dominating companies find it hard to change, the fossil record at Companies' House is full of once mighty firms, now deceased. For example, at the beginning of the last century, the economist Alfred Marshall drew up a list of the top 100 companies. So large and powerful were they, he argued that they would probably survive indefinitely. He referred to them as the Californian Redwoods: trees that can live for so long that, to us humans with our short life-span, they appear nearly immortal. Redwoods have been known to live for over 2,000 years. In 1999, the economist L. Hannah revisited the Marshall List, discovering that of the 100 largest firms in 1912, 29 had gone bankrupt, 48 had disappeared, and only 19 were still in the US Top 100.

Even the mighty fail, eventually. Disruptive technology combined with the inability of large firms, shackled and blinded by their network of expertise, all but guarantees it.

Give It the Boot

The study conducted by Christensen showed that the new products, the 5.25 inch or the 3.5 inch drives had an application at their outset. Specialisation was the key. For a product to be produced efficiently, the production process needs elements of specialisation; a network of expertise needs to be given time to form. To begin with, the new drives were not especially efficient or well designed, but they did have niche market applications, providing the oxygen for them to establish themselves. Supposing a new technology boasts the potential to yield outstanding benefits down the line, once specialisation has taken place, but in the short-run has no niche market for it to appeal to.

Consider the clever experiment of the programmer Danny Hillis.

He was testing how natural selection can work in a computer environment. He set a scenario in which he was trying to evolve a "number sorting program," using randomly created pieces of code. He programmed in the ability for code to mutate randomly and a system for affording survival to the code best suited to sorting numbers. To begin with, the code that appeared was pretty hopeless at the task it had been set. Very soon, however, programs evolved that became proficient at their job.

This came with a catch. No matter how many time Hillis ran the experiment, the code that eventually evolved was good, but not as good as code that could be developed by decent programmers. To resolve this, he came up with a truly clever solution. He introduced predator code into his system. This code attacked and swallowed up other code that had ceased to change. By doing this, Hillis forced a degree of randomness into the system, even when it was at a mature level.

But, by introducing predators, the various forms of code are forced to explore more alternatives: the odds of stumbling across the more optimal path increases. In network terms, once that network forms, once the hubs emerge, structure becomes established. It takes something quite radical to change that: the existing hubs must be destroyed. Sometimes, to move two steps forward, you need to first move one backwards. The innovator's dilemma illustrates how established firms cannot easily move backwards, where new companies can seize a new opportunity more effectively. Sometimes technology offers considerable opportunity. It can be necessary for an entire marketplace to first regress.

Renewable energy may well offer outstanding advantages over fossil fuels. In the long term, renewable energy may prove both cheaper and safer. At the moment this is patently not the case. Some are cynical, saying that once we run out of oil, we will rapidly return to the Stone Age.

Notably, fossil fuels have benefited from an investment over the years of trillions of dollars. Of course, renewables are currently inferior. They have neither benefited from that volume of investment, nor the specialisation that comes with it. The network has not yet been given time to form. Consider wind power: assuming we are not in danger of sapping the Earth's ability to generate wind, the many critics of wind power miss the point. They say it is inefficient; that on a calm day when wind speed is low, this form of power becomes useless. They are not taking into account the benefits that specialisation brings. The current generation of wind turbines are not optimal. The future might bring wind farms thousands of feet in the air anchored to the ground with cable. No one can yet say for sure how to optimally exploit wind power. Only through experimentation and through establishing a network of expertise can we learn.

Destruction Helps

When the network of the ecosystem of 65 million years or so ago existed, dinosaurs were so dominant that our evolutionary ancestors were scraping the bottom of the barrel for a living. When the meteorite struck the Yucatan Peninsula, that all changed. To become the world's dominant players, mammals needed the destruction afforded them by that meteorite. Sometimes radical, even wanton destruction is required to enable change. Destruction creates a vacuum; and into that vacuum new ideas emerge.

This is why the phrase "too big to fail" is an oxymoron. If a bank is so big as to convince people to believe that it should not fail, smaller banks are not being given a sufficient chance to evolve. "Too big to fail" really means "too big to permit evolution or development". "Too big" really means "inflexible," or "unadaptable," or "monolithic". This is the problem with the banking bailout of 2008–09. From one point of view, rescuing the banks was essential to save the hubs in the economic network. Indeed, studies have shown that banking crises have a tendency to create a cascade effect on the rest of the economy. During the peak of the 2008 banking crisis, former Scandinavian finance ministers advised the likes of Gordon Brown to bail out the banks. They were drawing upon their own experiences: Norway in 1989 and Sweden and Finland in 1991.They argued that because the government of that time chose to bail out the banks, the resulting contraction in GDP was much less severe than would have been the case had they been allowed to fail. But, on the other hand, a system made up of large dominant banks is resistant to change. Later, I demonstrate why such resistance has disastrous consequences.

Large-scale failure can, perversely, have positive benefits. The vacuum that is created enables new companies and entrepreneurs to develop ideas that could never compete against established players. In that space, new products and ideas become more sophisticated; ultimately they become superior to the product that they were initially unable to surpass.

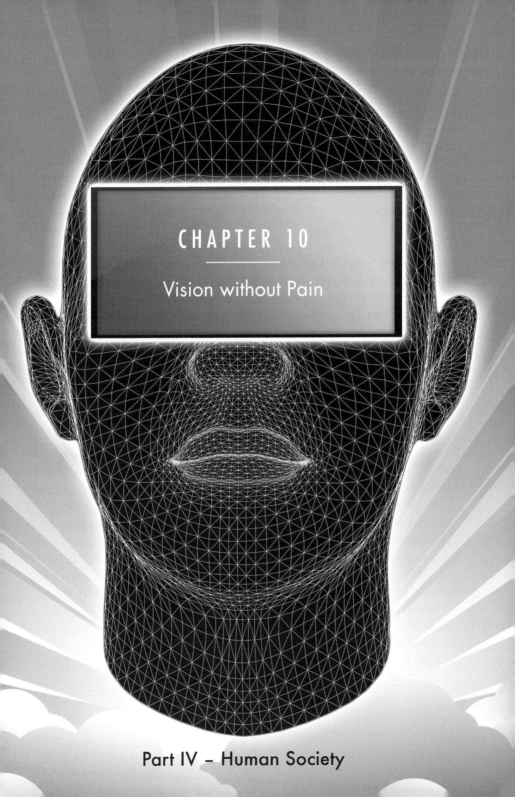

CHAPTER 10

Vision without Pain

Part IV – Human Society

CHAPTER 10

Vision without Pain

Economists like their laws. They like their equilibrium, and their theories of perfect competition and efficient markets. They will promote all kinds of theories to explain how economic policies caused this triumph or that victory, and how errors caused these problems or that disaster. Is it not possible that there are underlying forces at work? Is it not true that in comparison to these forces the actions of central bankers and the dictates of economic theorists are irrelevant? Was the Great Depression caused because central banks allowed the money supply to contract? Was it caused because governments made policy errors when trying to boost demand? What about 1970s inflation? Which government error caused that disaster? Was it spending on the war in Vietnam, a rising money supply, fluctuations in the supply of oil, or Trade Unions? As for the 2008–09 crash, was this down to mad bankers, regulatory groupthink or the return of greed?

Could it be that "nothing" is the correct answer?

I suggest a deeper underlying force is in play: the power of innovation. From the invention of dynamite in the late 1860s, to the launch of the iPhone, innovation is the key. Big ideas such as flight; small ideas such as the standardisation of the lids of polystyrene cups; these ideas have created economic growth. Innovation, and the implications thereof, is what shapes and drives the economy. Smil's Age of Symmetry 1867 and 1914, the golden era of innovation, described in Chapter 6, was a period of profound importance. The underlying cause of the Great Depression was that demand did not keep pace with the potential implicit in the innovations that preceded that period. Productivity rose, but wages didn't rise as fast, so the world fell into depression. The underlying cause of 1970s inflation was that we had finally caught up the potential created by previous innovations. Growth slowed down because we have become reliant on new innovation, but demand kept rising at the pace we had become used to.

---

[52] Scientist Falk Warnecke has been investigating termites and how they can solve the energy crisis, as reported by Julia Olmstead for Smithsonian.com.

The Forgotten Law

The law that economists forget is called Moore's Law. I don't mean that in its usual sense, suggesting that computers double in speed every 18 months. Rather I refer to it in its metaphorical sense, as short hand, for very rapid technological change. Today we are entering a new era of innovation, one that may surpass the late-Victorian pre-First World War period. As such, the ideas of economists from the last few decades may be obsolete: they were formed to describe a period when the world was nursing a hangover, earned during the party times of innovation catch-up.

The potential is everywhere to be seen. From nanotechnology to advances in genetics, from allowing new drugs to be safely evaluated without needing recourse to animal testing, through the synthetic cultivation of organs, to studying how termites convert cellulose into sugar allowing for new methods for creating biofuel without reducing agricultural output.[52]

In 1965, Gordon Moore at Intel predicted that the number of components on an integrated circuit would double every two years. His original prediction has been changed by popular mythology: today we say Moore's Law predicts computers will double in speed every 18 months. As we all know, computers do just that. The evidence is clear for everyone to see: the point is so important that I'll risk stating the obvious. The transformation of technology from a mainframe the size of a small house to a computer thousands of times more powerful that fits in our pocket is remarkable. If the average family saloon had seen its top speed rise at a trajectory consistent with Moore's Law since 1964, today we would be travelling at ten times the speed of light. This stunning change is not limited to computers. Today the human genome can be sequenced in a fraction of the time it once took to sequence that of the simplest living organism. Geneticist Craig Venter reckons he is close to building upon that knowledge to create an artificial organism that can convert carbon dioxide from the air to octane.

Consider 3D printing: a technology which allows three-dimensional objects to be visualised on two-dimensional material. Eventually, such technology may enhance manufacturing processes, making them faster and more efficient. It will make most jobs related to the manufacturing of those products obsolete.

Are you worried about a food crisis as our burgeoning population grows? How about this for a solution: vertical farms? As Dickson Despommier pointed out for *Scientific American*, just as high rise buildings have made it possible to pack more people into a limited area and make cities more densely populated, high-rise farms, built on multiple levels can enable us to grow much more food from the surface area of the Earth. Meanwhile, we are making great strides in developing machines controlled directly from our minds. Miguel A. L. Nicolelis told the story in *Scientific American* November 2009. All we have to do is think "move right", and the machine we are controlling moves right. Maybe, in time, touch typing will be replaced by thought typing. In another *Scientific American* article by Tim Folger, entitled "Contact: The Day After", it is argued that we can search a given area of space in less than a second that, a few years ago, would have taken over 200 hours. The article suggests that at the rate at which computing power increases, the task of searching the heavens becomes more efficient: electromagnetic signals emitted from an alien intelligence, should they exist, will be found within 30 years. In other words, if we ever discover evidence of alien intelligence, that evidence will be found during the first half of this century.

Nanotechnology is perhaps the most exciting of the lot. Among it's many applications is the potential to create new formations of carbon atoms: we can create molecules of any shape required. This would be a major breakthrough: carbon composites have a higher tensile strength than steel. As James Martin points out in his book *The Meaning of the 21st Century*, nanotechnology also provides the possibility of creating tiny switches, one hundredth the size of today's smallest transistors. This would give us the potential to make computers that much more powerful. Thanks to nanotechnology, in a decade or two, we may see a sharp acceleration in Moore's Law, as applied to computing capability.

What is especially interesting about nanotechnology is the potential that exists for nano-robots to evolve. The speed at which natural selection works is partially dependent on the time gap between each generation. A virus reproduces, and mutates, very quickly. This makes it extremely difficult for us to win the "war on viruses". In the same way, a piece of nanotechnology can reproduce and mutate much more quickly than even a biological virus, providing the potential for technological advances to outpace our current understanding.

In fact, James Martin reckons there are three stages of Darwinian evolution. Stage one is "primary evolution", the evolutionary process described by Darwin. It relates to the evolution of living species by natural selection. This stage is slow: it requires mutation to DNA to introduce change; this is the product of chance. Stage two is secondary evolution, which relates to cultural evolution and of ideas themselves, culminating perhaps in the ability to manipulate DNA. This second stage is faster than the first, because it builds on what we have already learned: it works by selecting and favouring ideas developed through deliberation. The third stage is what Martin calls "tertiary evolution": a phase we may be entering now. This occurs when intelligent beings learn how to automate evolution itself. To begin with, we see computer programmes built around artificial selection which follow parameters set down by a human creator; in time this process will accelerate, becoming very swift indeed.

In *Transforming the Twentieth Century: Technical Innovations of 1867–1914 and Their Lasting Impact* Vaclav Smil says: "The past six generations have amounted to the most rapid and the most profound change our species has experienced in its 5000 years of recorded history."

The next generation will probably witness more change than the previous six combined, as developments occur at an increasing rate. Old maxims about how it always takes years for new technology to gain momentum are no longer valid. So incredible are these opportunities that it is baffling that we should be so preoccupied with central bankers. In shaping the real forces that will impact upon us, they are about as important as Mickey Mouse.

A Bit of Science Fiction

But, just as we do well not to dismiss warnings because they have not yet been proven right, we should digress for a few paragraphs into the world of science fiction. Some of the more fanciful warnings of our imaginary future have not yet come to be; indeed, just because such warnings are the stuff of entertainment, lurking in kids' comics, it does not mean we should ignore them. For one thing the Internet can be a force for the exaggeration of our confirmation bias. The Internet, through channels such as Google and Facebook, focus on those things that interest us. As Eric Schmidt said when he was CEO at Google: "It will be very hard for people to watch or consume something that has not been in some sense tailored for them."

Schmidt's prediction may seem like good news. But if tools such as Google filter out sources of information that present ideas that differ from the group, then we will become even more set in our views. The danger lies in what Eli Pariser calls *The Filter Bubble*: which describes what happens when the Internet, thanks to the information it gains about us, feeds us what it thinks we want to know. So, if two different people type the same words into Google, they get quite different results. Pariser tried an experiment with two people, asking them to type "Egypt" into Google. One found that the first few results promoted Egypt as a tourism spot, the other had Egypt as a location of social unrest. At least, in the days when the gatekeepers of knowledge, the editors of newspapers and magazines, exercised a certain amount of discretion in what information was fed to us, there was an attempt at providing balance. The BBC has its critics, but its obsession with even-handedness, even if its editors are themselves biased in ways they may not be aware of, does at least attempt to promote objectivity.

The gatekeepers of the Internet are algorithms. So, while we may assume the internet will spread knowledge and understanding it may, in fact, act to reinforce our erroneous views.

Unfortunately, the problem runs deeper than that. Some argue that the Internet is changing the way we think. Nicholas Carr, in his book, *The Shallows*, argues that we are no longer capable of deep thinking: that we have become used to scanning for information. He says that our brains are in fact highly plastic, that the Internet has forced our neurons to rearrange in our lifetime, and that we are becoming increasingly unable to follow a complex argument.

"When the Net absorbs a medium, that medium is re-created in the Net's image," says Carr. "It injects the medium's content with hyperlinks, blinking ads, and other digital gewgaws, and it surrounds the content with the content of all the other media it has absorbed. A new e-mail message, for instance, may announce its arrival as we're glancing over the latest headlines at a newspaper's site. The result is to scatter our attention and diffuse our concentration." He adds: "The faster we surf across the Web – the more links we click and pages we view – the more opportunities Google and other companies gain to collect information about us and to feed us advertisements. Most of the proprietors of the commercial Internet have a financial stake in collecting the crumbs of data we leave behind as we flit from link to link – the more crumbs, the better. The last thing these companies want is to encourage leisurely reading or slow, concentrated thought. It's in their economic interest to drive us to distraction."

So, is the Internet in some way sapping our concentration? Even that danger is trivial compared to others.

Imagine a PC doubles in speed every 18 months. Imagine that PC finally matches the power of the human brain. Does that not mean that 18 months later it will be twice the speed of the human brain, and 30 years later, it will one million times the power of the human brain? If computers are designed by computers, then is it not reasonable to assume that, if a computer has twice the power of the human brain, it can design a computer that is twice as fast, in half the time it would have taken a human to achieve the same? A computer that is 32 times faster than a human brain, can double the speed of the computer it designs in 1./32nd of the time it would take that same human. To put it another way, within about 12 months of us designing a computer that is double the speed of the human brain, might we not have a computer than has near infinite capacity? Ray Kurzweil predicts, in his book *The Singularity is Near*, that this point, or something similar, will occur in 2045. There are snags with the theory. For one thing, the speed of a computer is determined by how small its chips are; there is a physical limit to how small things can be. Or, at least we think there is. However, suppose we become closer to our machines?

Carr quotes Sergey Brin, co-founder of Google as saying: "Certainly if you had all the world's information directly attached to your brain, or an artificial brain that was smarter than your brain, you'd be better off." Imagine if we could create a stronger interface between us and the Internet? Imagine that, in 30 years' time, computers are typically 1,000 times faster than they are today, and internet bandwidth speeds are 100 times faster. As Garry Stone pointed out for *Scientific American*, work is being done presently to see how information can be messaged directly into the brain.

How long will it be before we bypass the need for a computer sitting in our pocket, and instead we have one in our brain? "Silicon chip inside her head," as Bob Geldof once sang, connecting to the Internet at speeds way in excess of what is now possible. Would we need to learn a new language, or study maths, or would we merely download a program that does the work for us, on the fly?

Could we overcome the challenge of uploading ourselves into that computer? Nick Bostrom from Future of Humanity Institute at Oxford speculated thus; "Some human individuals upload and make many copies of themselves. Meanwhile, there is gradual progress in neuroscience and artificial intelligence, and eventually it becomes possible to isolate individual cognitive modules and connect them up to modules from other uploaded minds." he continued: "There might be multiple standards; some modules might specialize in translating between incompatible standards. Competitive uploads begin outsourcing increasing portions of their functionality: Why do I need to know arithmetic when I can buy time on Arithmetic–Modules Inc. whenever I need to do my accounts? Why do I need to be good with language when I can hire a professional language module to articulate my thoughts? Why do I need to bother with making decisions about my personal life when there are certified executive-modules that can scan my goal structure and manage my assets so as best to fulfil my goals?" He went on to say: "When it becomes possible to copy modules at will, to send high-bandwidth signals between parts of different brains, and to build architectures that cannot readily be implemented on biological neural nets, it might turn out that the optima relative to this new constraints-landscape have shifted away from the human-like mind region. There might be no niche for mental architectures of a human kind."

George Dyson, in *Darwin Among the Machines*, put it this way; "Everything that human beings are doing to make it easier to operate computer networks is at the same time, but for different reasons, making it easier for computer networks to operate humans."

Pitfalls of the Innovation Revolution

Above, it was told how technology is advancing at such a rapid rate, that the potential to create economic prosperity for all is very real. But there are pitfalls.

The Luddites were wrong, but only up to a point. As Dickens so brilliantly demonstrated, in the midst of the Industrial Revolution, poverty was rife.

Automation claimed its victims. We became better off in the long term, but hardship occurred en route. Looking forward, we face the same problem. It is quite hard to see where new jobs will come from when nanotechnology or 3D printing become commonplace. We are entering a new age in the knowledge economy: for those of us who have the required level of skill, this is an exciting development. But, for those who do not, it will be quite dangerous. This begs a question: will we create a new underclass?

There is danger that the trend we have seen in recent years of seeing income being less evenly distributed will become more extreme. It does appear that, on the whole, a lower birth rate is correlated with higher education and income levels. Conversely, in a society which sees a growing divide between those who are highly educated and the rest, there is also the danger that the population of the "haves" will fall, while the population of the "have nots" will rise. This is not an unavoidable problem but, in recent years, especially in the US, social mobility has fallen. If the network develops in such a way as to secure the position of those at the top of the league, in an environment in which education is the key to enjoying the fruits of opportunity, the divide between the rich and the rest will grow. But, the network is good at maintaining the status quo. The baby boomers and their media are reinforcing views that may have been appropriate a few decades ago, but which are not so relevant today.

Optimism is provided by research that shows intelligence levels seem to be both rising and becoming more equal. This phenomenon is known as the Flyn effect. For example, one test in Spain conducted over a thirty-year period, suggests that over that time frame, mean IQ increased by 9.7 points. However, there was little change at the top end: the significant increases were at the lower end of the scale.

This Time It Really is Different

We all know the story of the Boy Who Cried Wolf. We often take this story out of context. Each time he raised a false alarm, fewer villagers came to help him. When real danger loomed, no one came to his aid. The true lesson of Aesop's fable is that by ignoring the boy, the villagers lost out; their sheep were slaughtered. Can we really afford to ignore anyone who calls wolf? One day, they might just be right.

Some people shrug off fears regarding manmade climate change, because we were warned in the 1970s that an ice age was coming. Scientists may or may not be right about anthropogenic global warming. We simply cannot afford to ignore one warning because another has been proven wrong. No doubt, the pragmatic cynics among the people of Easter Island responded to those who warned that deforestation was not sustainable by saying: "Yes, yes. People said that to my grandfather too."

Bertrand Russell told the story of a chicken on a farm, which lived a life of blissful happiness. Recently Nassim Taleb updated the tale, but in his story it was a turkey. The turkey was looked after well by the farmer; the bird got fatter, and happier. How lucky it was. It laughed off the doubts cast about by other turkeys, that these good times could never last, that the farmer was not to be trusted. Then one day, the turkey blissfully allowed the hands of the farmer to grip it by the neck, unaware that the next day was Thanksgiving. Once again, this is the problem of induction. We form views based on insufficient evidence and, as the evidences supports our view, we become more certain we are right. However, we only need to be wrong once for all those beliefs to be destroyed. In the case of the turkey, a sense of understanding of its own fate may have served little benefit. But, for sentient beings as potent as us, a more insightful view is required.

Another saying, which bubble watchers like using is "this time it's different". This is ironic: the true meaning of "this time it is different" is "beware, for it is always the same". When people try to justify a booming stock market some say it's a "new paradigm now". But, say the cynics, it never is. Nothing ever changes. Is this not the secret of wisdom?

Traditionally, the holders of wisdom were the elders. Indeed, it is possible that the reason why we have evolved to allow some to live to a very old age is because the wisdom such longevity affords may promote the survival of a community.[53] Such wisdom is limited by the constraints of the network. It is fraught with the problem of induction. It is as if our experience, our knowledge, formed over the generations becomes hardwired into our understanding; this is a network that is indeed hard to change. Wisdom tells us that "there's nothing new under the sun," or "this time, it's no more different than last time".

But, this time, it is as different as it could possibly be.

The short period we have been on this planet has been largely characterised by accelerating change. Sure, there have been times when change has slowed down but, on the whole, it seems each revolution in technology has shortened the time it takes to reach the next one. For 95 per cent of *Homo sapiens'* existence we did not have farming, writing or cities. With each step forward, the gap to the next shortens. Here is a caveat: change is very hard to implement, but when it occurs, it can be very sudden indeed: we will have little control over it.

Most of us assume that water freezes at zero degrees Celsius. This is not true: if water is pure and undisturbed, it can be cooled to temperatures of −40°C. What happens at 0°C is that ice melts. There's a difference. Examine the super-cooling of water in the same terms as the Thanksgiving turkey. One water molecule says to the next, "I just don't believe this turning to ice nonsense. They said that when the temperature turned to zero we will all lock into position. But it hasn't happened? It's −10° now, but I am still free." However, once super-cooled water begins to freeze, it freezes immediately. So, the water molecule might have spoken thus: "Fears that we will freeze are exaggerated. All the evidence suggests that we will be ..." Alas, the molecule didn't quite get to finish its sentence.

Or the turkey may think: "I love this farmer. This place is great. I didn't know I was entitled to a Shiatsu ..."

---

53 Chris Stringer and Robin McKie, *African Exodus*, (London: Jonathan Cape, 1996), p. 198. "There would have been no point in having language if we did not have the power to retain the complicated knowledge that we wished to pass on. With good memories we would have been able to sustain complex social relations. We could recall where we saw good hunting grounds the previous year and where we could find food supplies and vegetation. Tied to the notion is the issue of longevity. If humans lived, on average, to an older age, we would have been able to pass on more cumulative wisdom stored in our memory banks. There would have been more elders to transmit the benefit of their knowledge: what had been done in their youths during serious drought, for example. In other words it was the rise of the human grandparent that gave our species its precious boost."

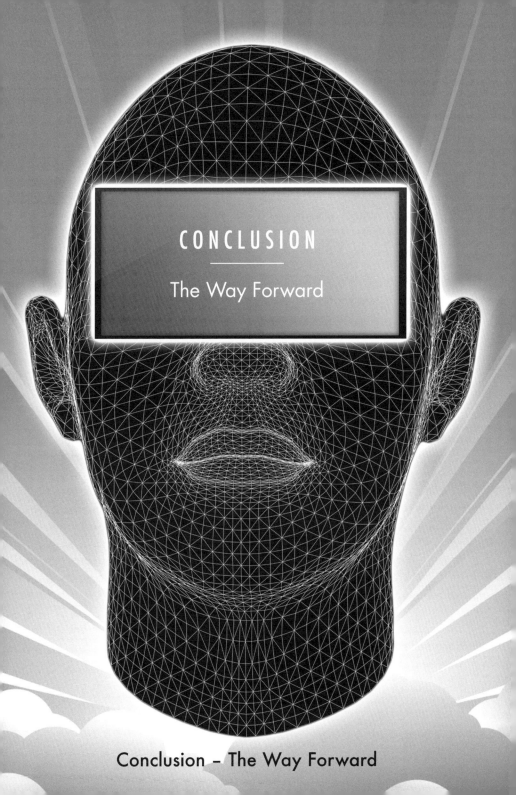

CONCLUSION

The Way Forward

Conclusion – The Way Forward

CONCLUSION

The Way Forward

So how do we manage the future? If there is one thing that the financial crisis of 2008–09 should have taught us, it is that the so-called experts are as much in the dark as the rest of us. It always amazes me how we take the word of an expert, applied to an area he or she may have no expertise in, and quote them as if it's gospel. We will not linger on science fiction for much longer, but this particular example is so amazing that I am going to mention it. As you know, we are sending signals out into space in an effort to communicate with alien intelligences that may be out there. Stephen Hawking has been widely quoted as saying that this is a bad idea insofar as there may be a gang of marauding aliens out there looking for planets to ransack. He may or may not be right: he is guessing. He may be very clever and have profound understanding of maths. This does not make him an expert on alien psychology.[54] As such everyone's view on this matter has equal credibility.

I do not have the solution to the dangers listed above. I do, however, have an idea on how we can find that solution. It lies in the superior intelligence groupthink can bring. The way forward is to harness the power of groupthink without letting our views become polarised, or worse still, let ourselves be blindly taken along by the group, safe in the knowledge that someone knows what's going on. Like the Californian sardines, finding it impossible to gather the collective intelligence to swim away from the shallow water they were stripping of oxygen, or like the people of Easter Island, convinced the practice they had followed for generations could not be their undoing. How then, can we rip off the blindfold and move the network away from acts of calamitous masochism?

The solution to enhancing groupthink without falling foul of its inherent dangers lies in more individualism. That's perhaps the most optimistic statement in this book.

---

[54] Does such an expert exist?

Michael Lewis goes a step further in the *Big Short*, where he attempts to provide psychological profiles of those traders who made money out of the financial crisis. He reckons that some of them had a rare neurological disorder, making it harder for them to empathise with others. Such people are often mistrustful, and had learnt to be more independent in their thinking; to rely on more objective measures. Others seemed to have strong anti-authoritarian feelings. The snag with these emotional characteristics is that such people may not be good at enhancing the power of the crowd. They are good at running against it which, from an investment point of view, may be useful for avoiding bubbles, but such an anti-crowd mentality would not be good for collaboration, demonstrated here as the very force that advances innovation.

Leonard Mlodinow talks about taming our biases, about how through education we can get a better grasp of probability and thus be less prone to making so many errors in the way we interpret numbers and patterns.

A paper by Linda Babcock and George Loewenstein examined ways to more effectively de-bias someone. In one experiment they asked subjects to take on the role of either plaintiff or defendant in a scenario involving a motorbike accident; the scenario was based on a real-life event. The subjects were randomly assigned their role, given identical information about the incident, and then asked to negotiate for 30 minutes to agree a settlement figure. They were given a financial incentive to agree this amount; in the event they were unable to agree, the settlement was determined by a "judge", but if they had to resort to settlement this way the reward received by the two players was reduced, to compensate for "legal fees". In other words, the subjects had been given an incentive to agree an "out of court" settlement. The researchers found that the two subjects found it hard to see the other's point of view. The subject's own expectations of the judge's award tended to favour their own position. So, plaintiffs typically expected the judge to award a higher settlement than defendants. To overcome this, Babcock and Loewenstein first asked subjects to read a passage about the self-serving bias. They even took a short test to ensure they understood what they had read. Despite, this the parties were just as influenced and estimated the judge's likely decision in their favour. Remarkably, however, subjects felt their opponents would be influenced by the self-serving bias, and that as a result would not be objective. To put it in the words of Babcock and Loewenstein: "Our results indicate that informing subjects of the bias made them more realistic about the predictions of the other party. However, it did not cause them to modify their own prediction of the judge. When they learned about the bias, subjects apparently assumed that the other person would succumb to it, but did not think it applied to themselves."

The researchers then tried asking their subjects to write an essay arguing their opponent's case. Remarkably, this has the effect of reinforcing their view. By forcing subjects to make a better effort to understand this opposite point of view, their initial judgement of their own position was actually strengthened. Finally, they asked subjects to focus on their own judgement and to try and pick flaws in their own arguments.

By doing this, the researchers found both subjects developed a more realistic view of what judgement would be made; incidents of impasse when the decision was made by the judge reduced from 35 to just 4 per cent.

Earlier, we examined the various biases that haunt us all. Another bias that is typically most annoying, unless that is it's us who are practising it, is the hindsight bias. "Of course I always knew that was going to happen." Or, "As I predicted; it's turned out precisely how I expected."

In the classic study carried out by Baruch Fischhoff in 1975, two obscure events in history were described to people. Then four possible outcomes were outlined, and subjects were asked which was the most likely? Subjects gave various answers, assigning different levels of probability to each possible outcome. A second group of subjects were first told what the final outcome was and then asked which of the four outcomes were most likely. It probably won't surprise you to learn that in cases when subjects knew what the actual outcome was, they assigned a much higher degree of likelihood to that outcome than the other three possible outcomes. But, in such situations, we are being dishonest with ourselves. We may look at an unravelling series of events, see certain occurrences as inevitable and then describe patterns which are false. Groupthink is therefore wrong when we look back at certain scenarios through the prism of hindsight in order to establish rules to describe how things will work in the future. Those rules end up being false.

Various studies have looked into how people can be encouraged to overcome the hindsight bias. The technique that seemed to work best involved asking subjects to consider the circumstances that could lead to an alternative outcome. It seems that in order to overcome our bias, we must consider scenarios which force us to closely examine the position we have taken. The confirmation bias might be conquered by working harder to think of ways we may be wrong; this is not as easy as it seems. Working against the confirmation bias requires a degree of self-discipline that few of us have been able to implement. The Oracle of Ancient Delphi once said Socrates was the wisest man in the world; Socrates believed a wise man was one who understood the degree of his ignorance. The philosopher may have been a rare example of an individual who had made progress in overcoming the confirmation bias. The two people who others look up to when the subject of bias come up are Daniel Kahneman and Amos Tversky. Tversky died in 1996, but Kahneman is still with us, and even won a Nobel Memorial Prize for Economics in 2002, without having ever taken an economics course. In "Judgment Under Uncertainty: Heuristics and Biases", Tversky and Kahneman, along with their co-editor Paul Slovic: said: "There is little experimental evidence that the hindsight bias is reduced by the sort of intense involvement with a topic that comes with a professional education."

There is both a problem and a benefit to being educated as to how to reduce our tendency to biases. Education that teaches us to be cynical and questioning can work, through forcing us to practice the various habits that can enable us to avoid a bias. An education that teaches us to accept everything we are told can be counter-productive. Equally, teamwork is important too. So somehow we have to learn how to both work as a team, and question the team.

It is clear that groups can be very effective when there is cross-fertilisation. Perhaps groupthink might be more effective when the group has its share of iconoclasts. It does seem that schools often have the effect of making kids conform; if you have children you may share this view. Individual thinking is often discouraged; essays which take an alternative point of view are slated by teachers. What education really needs to do is to train us to question. Teachers, the group, conventional wisdom: all of it.

The teaching of history is quite shocking. The national curriculum may be to blame. Kids are told to focus on the minutia of the clothes they wore in Ancient Greece; as a result they can lose sight of the big picture. If more economists had studied economic history, perhaps they would have seen the credit bubble in making. Instead the teaching of economic history is dwindling. Take this passage, taken from Norbert Häring's article in *Handelsblatt*, the German equivalent of the *FT*, translated by Amos Witztum, Professor of Economics, Secretary of ESHET: "Now, history of economic thought and general economic history are threatened with being completely cut off from the funds that subsidize research. The European Research Council (ERC), the most important source of academic research funding in Europe, with an annual budget of over a billion euros, has issued new guidelines for applicants. The 'panel descriptors' which tell applicants to which panel they should direct their application do not include history of economic thought or general economic history any more. There are only entries for history of institutions and for quantitative economic history."

In short, economists, still beguiled by the metaphors that define their subject, and seduced by that which can only be described as "physics envy", are turning their back on the one aspect of their discipline that could throw light on the underlying forces that shape the world; even when so many of their ideas have been discredited.

Only by education that teaches us to think for ourselves, education that teaches us to question teachers and their received wisdom, only by education that encourages individualism, multi-disciplinary studies, and only then via cross-fertilisation, can individualistic free thinkers using the enhanced Internet as their tool, learn how to exploit the power of groupthink. Then, and only then, can we strip off the network's blindfold, grapple with some of the hugely complex problems discussed in this book, and turn potential disaster into something truly magnificent.

BIBLIOGRAPHY

BIBLIOGRAPHY

AHN, Fish die-off in Ventura Harbor as sardines, anchovies lose oxygen from overcrowding, http://www.dbune.com/news/offbeat/5595-fish-die-off-in-ventura-harbor-as-sardines-anchovies-lose-oxygen-from-overcrowding.html, 13 May 2011

Akerlof, George A. and Kranton, Rachel. *Identity Economics*, Princeton University Press, Princeton, 2010

Akerlof, George A. and Shiller, Robert J. *Animal Spirits*, Princeton University Press, Princeton, 2009

Albert, Réka; Jeong, Hawoong; Barabási, Albert-László. "Attack and error tolerance of complex network", *Nature*, Vol 406: 378-382

Amalrik, Andrei. *Will the Soviet Union survive until 1984?* Harper and Row, 1970

Ariely, Dan. *Predictably irrational*, Harper, 2009

Asch, S. E. (1956). "Studies of independence and conformity: A minority of one against a unanimous majority". *Psychological Monographs*, 70 (Whole no. 416)

Babcock, Linda and Loewenstein, George. "Explaining Bargaining Impasse: The Role of Self-Serving Biases". *Journal of Economic Perspectives*. 11, pp. 109-126

Baker, Dean, "The President as Storyteller-in-Chief", http://rwer.wordpress.com/2011/02/14/the-president-as-storyteller-in-chief/, 13 May 2011

Ball, Philip. *Critical mass*, Arrow Books, 2005

Barabási, Albert-László, *Linked*, Penguin Books, London 2003

Battiston, S.; Gatti, D. D.; Gallegati, M.; Greenwal, B. C. N. and Stiglitz, J. E. (2009) "Liaisons Dangereuses: increasing Connectivity, Risk Sharing, and Systemic Risk" Working paper

Baxter, Michael and Herskind, Kenn. *Bubbles and Wisdom*, Asenta, London, 2009

Beinhocker, Eric D., *The Origin of Wealth, Evolution, complexity and radical remaking of economics*, Random House, London, 2005

Biever, Celeste. "Free trade may have finished off Neanderthals", *New Scientist*, 01 April 2005

Blalock, Garrick; Kadiyali, Vrinda; and Simon, Daniel H. "The Impact of 9/11 on Road Fatalities: The Other Lives Lost to Terrorism" (February 10, 2005)

Bond, Rod; Smith, Peter, B. "Culture and Conformity: A Meta-Analysis of Studies Using Asch's", *Psychologica Bulletin –1996* by the American Psychological Association, Inc. 1996. Vol. 119, No. I, pp. 111-137

Bootle, Roger. *Money for nothing*, Nicholas Brealey Publishing, London, 2005

Bostrom, Nick. Future of Humanity Institute, Faculty of Philosophy & James Martin 21st Century School, University of Oxford

Breedlove, William; Burkett, Tracy; Winfield, Idee. 2004 Collaborative Testing and Test Performance, http://www.rapidintellect.com/AEQweb/mo2609j4.htm, May 27 2011

Brown, Lester. R, *World on the Edge: How to Prevent Environmental and Economic Collapse*, W. W. Norton & Company, New York, January 6, 2011

Buller, David J. 'Evolution of the Mind: 4 fallacies of evolution', *Scientific American* December 2008

Calvin, William H. *How Brains Think*, Weidenfeld and Nicolson, London, 1996

Carr, Nicholas. *The Shallows: What the Internet is Doing to Our Brains*, W. W. Norton & Company (June 6, 2011)

CEBR, "Biggest peacetime squeeze on household disposable incomes since 1921", 11 April 2011

Christakis, Nicholas and Fowler, James. *Connected, the amazing power of social networks and how they shape our lives*, Harper Press, London 2011

Clinton, Bill. The White House, The East Room, June 26, 2000

Coghlan, Andy. "Thoughts of religion prompt acts of punishment", *New Scientist*, 24 November 2010

Colom, R.; Lluis-Font, J. M.; Andrés-Pueyo, A. (2005). "The generational intelligence gains are caused by decreasing variance in the lower half of the distribution: Supporting evidence for the nutrition hypothesis"

Congdon, Tim. *Keynes, the Keynesians and Monetarism*, Edward Elgar Publishing Ltd; illustrated edition edition (29 Aug 2007),

Cowie, Ian. "A tax-based alternative to the Alternative Vote", *Daily Telegraph*, 5 May 2011, http://blogs.telegraph.co.uk/finance/ianmcowie/100010127/a-tax-based-alternative-to-the-alternative-vote/ 27 May 2011

Coyle, Diane. *The Soulful Science*, Princeton University Press, Woodstock, 2007

Darwin, Charles. *The Autobiography of Charles Darwin* by the Classic British Free Public Domain Book from the Classic Literature Library http://charles-darwin.classic-literature.co.uk/the-autobiography-of-charles-darwin/ May 27 2011

Dawkins, Richard. *The Blind Watchmaker*, Penguin, London 1996

Dawkins, Richard. *The Selfish Gene*, Oxford University Press, Oxford, 1976

de Haan, Willem; Pijnenburg, Yolande A. L.; Strijers, Rob L. M., van der Made, Yolande; van der Flier, Wiesje M Scheltens; Philip; Stam, Cornelis J. "Functional neural network analysis in frontotemporal dementia and Alzheimer's disease using EEG and graph theory", *BMC Neuroscience*, Volume 10, Number 1, 101, DOI: 10.1186/1471-2202-10-101

Department of Computer Science University of York, EME: Biological Examples 1: slime moulds, http://www-course.cs.york.ac.uk/eme/7EMEBioEgs.pdf, 13 May 2011

Despommier, Dickson. "Growing Skyscrapers: The Rise of vertical farms" *Scientific American*, November 2009

Diamond, Jared. *Collapse*, Penguin Books, London, 2005

Diamond, Jared. *Guns, Germs and Steel*, Vintage Books, London 2005

Dimson, Elroy; Marsh, Paul; Staunton, Mike. "Irrational Optimism" http://zonecours.hec.ca/documents/E2008-1-1629825.texte5irrationaloptimism.pdf, 13 May 2011

Discover Small Business Watch, June 2007

Drucker, Peter F. *Modern Prophets: Schumpeter or Keynes?* http://www.druckersociety.at/files/p_drucker_proph_en.pdf 27 May 2011

Dugatkin, Lee Alan. *Inclusive Fitness Theory from Darwin to Hamilton*, Department of Biology, University of Louisville, Louisville, Kentucky 40241, http://www.genetics.org/content/176/3/1375.full 28 May 2011

Dunbar, Robin. *Grooming, Gossip and the evolution of language*, Faber and Faber, London, 2004

Dunbar, Robin. *How Many Friends Does One Person Need?: Dunbar's Number and Other Evolutionary Quirks*, Faber and Faber, 2011

Dyson, George. *Darwin Among the Machines*, Basic Books; 1st edition (October 8, 1998)

"Economic & Labour Market Review", Vol 4, No 8 August 2010, Office for National Statistics

Eggertsson, Gauti. "The Paradox of Toil", Federal Reserve Bank of New York Staff Reports February 2010 Number 433, http://www.newyorkfed.org/research/staff_reports/sr433.pdf May 27 2011

Eli Pariser. *The Filter Bubble: What the Internet Is Hiding from You*. Penguin Press HC, The (May 12, 2011)

Epstein J. and Axtell, R. *Growing Artificial Societies: Social Science from the Bottom Up*, MIT Press; First edition (29 Nov 1996)

Ernst and Young "UK households 15% worse off than 5 years ago" http://www.ey.com/UK/en/Newsroom/News-releases/Retail—08-07-04—UK-households-worse-off May 29 2011

Faloutsos, M.; Faloutsos, P.; Faloutsos, C. (1999). "On power-law relationships of the internet topology". Comp. Comm. Rev. 29: 251

Feelgood Theosophy. *Robert Johnson. Did this Legendary Bluesman really make a pact with the Devil? & Why at a Crossroads?* http://blavatskyblogger.freeukisp.co.uk/feelgoodrobertjohnson.htm 27 May 2011

Fisk, Catherine L. *Working Knowledge: Employee Innovation and the Rise of Corporate Intellectual Property*, 1800-1930 (Studies in Legal History) The University of North Carolina Press October 9, 2009

Flynn, J. R. (2007). *What is Intelligence?: Beyond the Flynn Effect.* Cambridge University Press

Folger, Tim. "Contact: The Day After", http://www.scientificamerican.com/article.cfm?id=contact-the-day-after

Forsyth, Donelson R. "Group Dynamics", Wadsworth, Cengage Learning, 2009 http://www.cengagebrain.com/shop/content/forsyth99522_0495599522_01.01_toc.pdf, May 27 2011

Fukuyama, Francis. *Trust: The Social Virtues and the Creation of Prosperity*, Free Press; 1st edition August 1, 1995

Furnham, Adrian, "Thinking about intelligence", *The Psychologist* Vol 13 No 10, http://www.thepsychologist.org.uk/archive/archive_home.cfm/volumeID_13-editionID_49-ArticleID_148-getfile_getPDF/thepsychologist%5Cfurnham.pdf, 13 May 2011

Furnham, A.; Hosoe, T.; and Tang, T. "Male hubris and female humility? A cross-cultural study of ratings of self, parental and sibling multiple intelligence in America, Britain and Japan". *Intelligence*, January 2002

Galbraith, John Kenneth. *The Great Crash 1929*, Penguin Books, London, 1954

Gigerenzer, Gerd. *Rationality for Mortals: How People Cope with Uncertainty*, Chapter 6, Out of the frying pan into the fire, Oxford University Press, 2008

Glick, J. C. and Staley, K. (2007). "Inflicted traumatic brain injury: Advances in evaluation and collaborative diagnosis". *Paediatric Neurosurgery*, 43, pp. 436–441

Goldberg, Andrew. "Patent defendants aren't copycats. So who's the real inventor here?" http://thepriorart.typepad.com/the_prior_art/2009/02/copying-in-patent-law.html 27 May 2011

Gould, Stephen J. and Eldredge, Niles. "Punctual equilibrium: the tempo and mode of evolution reconsidered". *Paleobiology*, 3 (2): 115-151, p 145

Gouliquer, Lynne. "Pandora's Box: The Paradox of Flexibility in Today's Workplace", *Current Sociology* January 2000 vol. 48 no. 1 29-38 http://csi.sagepub.com/content/48/1/29.abstract, 27 May 2011

Grand, Steve. "Where do those damn atoms go?", January 12 2009, http://stevegrand.wordpress.com/2009/01/12/where-do-those-damn-atoms-go/, May 13 2011

Greenspan, Alan. *The Age of Turbulence*, Allen Lane, London 2007

Greenspan. Alan, Speech to the Economic Club of New York (1988)

Guryan, Jonathan and Kearney, Melissa S. Gambling at Lucky Stores: Empirical Evidence from State Lottery Sales: faculty.chicagobooth.edu/jonathan.guryan/research/guryan_kearney_gambling_lucky_stores.pdf (22 August 2009)

Haldane, Andrew G., Rethinking the financial network, http://www.bankofengland.co.uk/publications/speeches/2009/speech386.pdf, 13 May 2011

Haldane, J. B. S., "1955 Population genetics". New Biol. 18: 34–51

Hall, Alfred Rupert. Philosophers at War: The Quarrel between Newton and Leibniz, Cambridge University Press (12 Sep 2002)

Häring, Norbert. article in Handelsblatt, the German equivalent of the FT, translated by Amos Witztum, Professor of Economics, Secretary of ESHET Real-World Economics Review, "The end of history in economics", http://rwer.wordpress.com/2011/03/24/the-end-of-history-in-economics/, May 13 2011

Hawking, Stephen. Does God play dice?, http://www.hawking.org.uk/index.php/lectures/64, 28 May 2011

Hiscox, "Creativity + networking + risk-taking = business success, say UK's graduates", 28 September, http://www.hiscox.com/news/press-releases/2010/28-09-2010.aspx 30 may 2011

Hölldobler, Bert and Wilson, Edward O. The Ants, Harvard University Press, 1990

Hollis, Martin. Reason in Action, Essays in the Philosophy of Social Science, Cambridge University Press, 26 January 1996

Hoppe, Hans-Hermann. The Misesian Case against Keynes, http://mises.org/daily/2492, May 27 2011

Horizon: Are We Still Evolving? was on BBC Two at 2100 on Tuesday 1 March 2011 http://www.cebr.com/wp-content/uploads/UK-Prospects-Press-Release-Apr-2011.pdf 27 May 2011 http://www.enotalone.com/article/6227.html, 10 May 2011

Hulme, David. An Enquiry Concerning Human Understanding, P. F. Collier & Son, 1910 (first published 1748)

Hutton, Will. Them and Us: Changing Britain – Why We Need a Fair Society, Little, Brown & Company, September 2010

IEO, "IMF Performance in the Run-Up to the Financial and Economic Crisis IMF Surveillance in 2004–07", http://www.ieo-imf.org/eval/complete/pdf/01102011/ IEO_full_report_crisis.pdf, May 27 2011 IMF THE INFLUENCE OF CREDIT DERIVATIVE AND STRUCTURED CREDIT MARKETS ON FINANCIAL STABILITY – Chapter II

Janis, I. L. (1972). *Victims of groupthink: A psychological study of foreign policy decisions and fiascoes*. Boston: Houghton Mifflin Company.

Johnson, Steven. *Emergence*, Penguin Books, London, 2001

Johnson. Steven *Where Good ideas come from*, Allen Lane, London, 2010

Journal of Personality and Social Psychology, Vol 32(6), Dec 1975, pp. 951-955

Kahneman and Miller (1986) "Norm Theory: Comparing reality to its alternatives", *Psychological Review*, 80, pp. 136-153

Kahneman, D.; Knetsch J. L; Thaler, R. H. "Experimental tests of the endowment effect and the Coase theorem". *Journal of Political Economy* 1990

Kahneman, D.; Knetsch J. L.; Thaler, R. H. "Anomalies: The endowment effect, loss aversion, and status quo bias". *The Journal of Economic Perspectives*, 1991

Kahneman, Daniel; Riepe, Mark W. "Aspects of Investor Psychology", *Journal of Portfolio Management*, Vol. 24 No. 4

Kahneman, Daniel; Slovic, Paul; Tversky, Amos,(edited by) *Judgment under uncertainty: heuristics and biases*, Cambridge University Press, Cambridge, 1982

Kandaswamy, Anand, *The Newton/Leibniz Conflict in Context*, http://www.math.rutgers. edu/courses/436/Honors02/newton.html, May 27 2011

Kealey, Terence. *Sex, Science and Profits*, William Heinemann: London, 2008

Keynes, John Maynard. *The General Theory of Employment, Interest and Money*, Atlantic Publishing, 2007. (First published 1935)

King, Mervyn. Comments on "Risk and Uncertainty in Monetary Policy" by Alan Greenspan, annual conference, 2004 http://www.bankofengland.co.uk/publications/ speeches/2004/speech209.pdf, May 27 2011

King, Mervyn. Lecture to the Society of Business Economists, London, 2 May 2007

Koch, Richard and Lockwood, Greg. *Superconnect*. Little, Brown, London, 2010

Kurzweil, Ray. *The Singularity Is Near: When Humans Transcend Biology*. Penguin (Non-Classics) 26 September 2006

Lakoff, George and Johnson, Mark. *Metaphors We Live By*, University of Chicago Press; New edition edition (1 May 1981)

Lamm, H., & Myers, D. G. *Group-induced Polarization of Attitudes and Behavior, Advances in Experimental Social Psychology*, 11, Academic Press, New York, pp. 145-195, 1978

Langer, Ellen J.; Roth, Jane. "Heads I win, tails it's chance: The illusion of control as a function of the sequence of outcomes in a purely chance task", *Journal of Personality and Social Psychology* (1975) Volume: 32, Issue: 6, pp. 951-955

Large, Sir Andrew, At the London School of Economics – "Financial Stability Oversight, Past & Present", Thursday 22 January 2004,http://www.bankofengland.co.uk/publications/speeches/2004/speech212.pdf, 13 May 2011

Leakey, Richard. *The Origin of Humankind*, Phoenix, London, 1994

Lehmann Laurent, and Feldman, Marc; of Stanford University. "War and The Evolution Of Belligerence And Bravery", *Medical News Today*, 27 August 2008

Levie, Jonathan; Hart Mark; and Karim, Mohammed Shamsul. Global Entrepreneurship Monitor, Impact of Media on Entrepreneurial Intentions and Actions, GEM UK project, http://www.bis.gov.uk/assets/biscore/enterprise/docs/I/11-773-impact-of-media-entrepreneurial-intentions-actions 30 May 2011

Lovelock, James. *Gaia*, Oxford University Press, Oxford, 1979

Macleod, Christine (1999), "Negotiating the Rewards of Invention: The Shop-Floor Inventor in Victorian Britain", *Business History*, Taylor and Francis Journals

Main E. C. and Walker, T. G. "Choice shifts and extreme behaviour – judicial review in the Federal courts", *Journal of Psychology* Volume 91 December 1973

Marshall, Jessica, "Gripping Yarns", *New Scientist* 12 February 2011

Martin, James. *The Meaning of the 21 Century*, Transworld Publishers, London 2006

May, R. M. (1974), *Stability and Complexity in Model Ecosystems*, Princeton University Press.

May, R. M. (2006), "Network structure and the biology of populations", *Trends in Ecology and Evolution* Vol. 27, No. 7.

Mayell, Hillary. "Genghis Khan a Prolific Lover, DNA Data Implies" *National Geographic* 14 January http://news.nationalgeographic.com/news/2003/02/0214_030214_genghis.html

MacAndrew, Alec. "FOXP2 and the Evolution of Language", www.evolutionpages.com/FOXP2_language.htm, 2 August 2011

McClure, Sam; Li, Jian; Tomlin, Damon; Cypert, Kim; Montague, Latane; Montague, Read. "Neural Correlates of Behavioral Preference for Culturally Familiar Drinks" *Neuron*, Volume 44, Issue 2, 379-387, 14 October 2004

McCrone, John, *The Ape that Spoke*, Macmillan London Ltd, London, 1990

McIntyre, Michael E. 2000, "Goodhart's law", http://www.atm.damtp.cam.ac.uk/mcintyre/papers/LHCE/goodhart.html, 25 May 2011

McKinsay Global. "Farewell to cheap capital? The implications of long-term shifts in global investment and saving", December 2010 http://www.mckinsey.com/mgi/publications/farewell_cheap_capital/pdfs/MGI_Farewell_to_cheap_capital_full_report.pdf, May 27 2011

McKinsey Global Institute. "Accounting for the cost of health care in the United States". New York: McKinsey and Company, 2007

Milgram, Stanley. "The Small-world-problem", *Psychology Today* 1967, pp. 61-67

Mithen, Steven. *The Prehistory of the Mind*, Phoenix, London, 1996

Mlodinow, Leonard. *The Drunkard's Walk*, Pantheon, 2008

Morris, Ian. *Why the West rules for now*, Profile Books, 2010

Moscovici, S. and Zavalloni, M. "The group as a polarizer of attitudes". *Journal of Personality and Social Psychology*, 12, pp. 125-135. (1969).

Moy, Dambisa. *How The West Was Lost*, Allen Lane, London

Moyer, Michael. "Religious Thought, Origins Issue of" *Scientific American*, August 2009

Mulholland, Hélène; and Vasagar, Jeevan. "Forced on to back foot over premium rate university places", *guardian.co.uk*, Tuesday 10 May 2011

Mullins, Justin. "Memristor Minds: The Future of Artificial Intelligence", *New Scientist* 8 July 2009

Nelson, Kevin. *The God Impulse: Is Religion Hardwired into the Brain?* Simon & Schuster Ltd, 3 March 2011

Newman, Mark. *Networks an introduction*, Oxford University Press, Oxford, 2010,

Nicolelis Miguel A. L. "Mind Out of Body: Controlling Machines with Thought" *Scientific American*, February 2011

Nicolelis, Miguel A. L. and Ribeiro, Sidarta. "Seeking the Neural Code", *Scientific American*, November 2006

Nouriel Roubini, *Crisis Economics*, Allen Lane London, 2010

Ogburn, William F. and Thomas, Dorothy. "Are Inventions Inevitable? A Note on Social Evolution", *Political Science Quarterly*, Vol. 37, No. 1 (Mar., 1922), pp. 83-98 http://www.jstor.org/pss/2142320

Olmstead, Julia. "Termite Bellies and Biofuel", Smithsonian.com, August 01, 2008 New Scientist 13 June 2009

Ormerod, Paul, *Why most things fail*, Faber and Faber, London 2005

Page, Scott E. The *Difference: How the Power of Diversity Creates Better Groups, Firms, Schools and Societies*, Princeton University Press, 2008

Parikh, Chetan, "The illusion of control, capital ideas online", http://www.capitalideasonline.com/articles/index.php?id=3056, 13 May 2011

Pinker, Steven. *The stuff of thought*, Penguin Books, London 2007

Pop Crunch, Bankrupt! 65 Famous People Who Lost It All, http://www.popcrunch.com/bankrupt-65-famous-people-who-lost-it-all/ 28 May 2011

Pugh, Peter. *Introducing Keynesian Economics*, Totem Books, 2000

Putnam, Robert D. *Making Democracy Work: Civic Traditions in Modern Italy*, Princeton University Press, May 27, 1994

Quiggin, John. *Zombie Economics*, Lines Princeton University Press, Woodstock, 2010

Radford, Peter, "The problem with physics, (On economics, influence of Physics and uncertainty)" http://rwer.wordpress.com/2011/03/06/the-problem-with-physics/, 13 May 2011

Rajan, Raghuram G. *Fault Lines* Princeton University Press, Woodstock, 2007

Ratey, John J. *Massive Cell Death, Part 2*. A User's Guide to the Brain: Perception, Attention, and the Four Theaters of the Brain

Reich, Robert B. "John Maynard Keynes", *Time magazine*, 29 March 2009,

Reinhart, Carmen M. and Rogoff, Kenneth S. *This time it is different*, Princeton University Press, Woodstock, 2009

Reisman, David A. *Schumpeter's market Enterprise and Evolution*, Edward Elgar Publishing, 2004

Reuters. "Millions of dead sardines found in Californian Marina", *The Guardian*, Tuesday 8 March 2011

Ridley, Matt. *The Rational Optimist, how prosperity evolves*, Fourth estate, London, 2010

Robson, David. "Disorderly genius: How chaos drives the brain", *New Scientist,* 29 June 2009

Romer, Paul. "Post-Scarcity Prophet Economist Paul Romer on growth, technological change, and an unlimited human future", *Reason online*, December 2001: www.reason.com/news/show/28243.html 25 August 2009

Sample, Ian. "Near-death experiences reveal how our brains work", *The Observer*, Sunday 13 March 2011

Schelling, T. (1969). "Models of segregation", *The American Economic Review*, 1969, 59(2), pp. 488-493

Shaw, Marjorie E. from Columbia University, "A Comparison of Individuals and Small Groups in the Rational Solution of Complex Problems", *American Journal of Psychology*, volume 44, number 3, July 1932

Sherif, M. (1935). "A study of some social factors in perception". *Archives of Psychology*, 27

Shermer, Michael. "How Randomness Rules Our World and Why We Cannot See It", *Scientific American Magazine*, October 2008

Smil, Vaclav. *Creating the Twentieth Century: Technical Innovations of 1867-1914 and Their Lasting Impact.* Oxford: Oxford University Press 2005

Smith, Adam. *Wealth of Nations,* A Selected Edition (Oxford World Classics), 2008

Smithies, Arthur. "Schumpeter and Keynes", *The Review of Economics and Statistics,* Vol. 33, No. 2 (May, 1951), pp. 163-169

Soros, George. Theory of Reflexivity MIT Speech, Laboratory Conference Washington, D.C, Delivered April 26, 1994

Stein, Matthew. *When Technology Fails: A Manual for Self-Reliance, and planetary survival*

Sterelny, Kim. *Dawkins vs. Gould, Survival of the fittest,* Icon Books, Ltd, Cambridge, 2001

Stone, Garry H. "Jacking into the Brain". *Scientific American* Nov, 2008

Stone, James A. F. "Risky and cautious shifts in group decisions", *Journal of Experimental Social Psychology,* Volume 4, Issue 4, October 1968, pp. 442-459 Massachusetts Institute of Technology

Stringer, Chris and McKie, Robin. *African Exodus,* Jonathan Cape, London, 1996

Surowiecki, James. *The Wisdom of Crowds: Why the Many Are Smarter Than the Few and How Collective Wisdom Shapes Business, Economies, Societies and Nations,* Doubleday 2004,

Svenson, O. (1981). Are we less risky and more skillful than our fellow drivers? Acta Psychological, 47, 143-151. See also Running head: COMPARATIVE EVALUATION When Good = Better Than Average Don A. Moore Carnegie Mellon University http://www.cbdr.cmu.edu/papers/pdfs/cdr_029.pdf. 28 May 2011

Tainter, Joseph. *The Collapse of Complex Societies,* Cambridge University Press, Cambridge, U.K.

Taleb, Nassim Nicholas. *Fooled by Randomness,* Penguin, London 2007

Taleb, Nassim Nicholas. *The Black Swan,* Penguin Books, London, 2007

Tversky, Amos; Kahneman, Daniel. "Judgment under Uncertainty: Heuristics and Biases", *Science, New Series,* Vol. 185, No. 4157. (Sep. 27, 1974), pp. 1124-1131

Tversky, Amos; Kahneman, Daniel. "The Framing of Decisions and the Psychology of Choice", *Science, New Series,* Vol. 211, No. 4481. (Jan. 30, 1981), pp. 453-458.

Venter, Craig. Annual Richard Dimbleby Lecture for the BBC in December 2007 www.bbc.co.uk/pressoffice/pressreleases/stories/2007/12_december/05/ dimbleby.shtml, 7 June 2011

vos Savant, Marilyn. "Game Show Problem" *Parade Magazine*, 1990 http://www. marilynvossavant.com/articles/gameshow.html. 28 May 2011

Vrba, E. S. (1993), "The pulse that produced us" *National History* 102 (5), pp. 47-51

Waggoner, Ben and Speer B. R. Introduction to the "Slime Molds", http://www.ucmp. berkeley.edu/protista/slimemolds.html, May 13 2011

Watts, D. (2002), "A simple model of global cascades on random networks", *Proceedings of the National Academy of Sciences* 9: 5766-5771.

Watts, D. J. and Strogatz, S. H. (1998), "Collective dynamics of 'small-world" networks', *Nature 393* (6684): 409–10.

Westerhoff, Nikolas. "Set in Our Ways: Why Change Is So Hard", *Scientific American Mind* (December 17, 2008)

Wilder, Rebecca. "It's not structural unemployment, it's the corporate saving glut", http://www.angrybearblog.com/2011/03/its-not-structural-unemployment-its.html May 27 2011

Wilson, Steve. "Duality solved?", *New Scientist*, 7 April 2010,

Wright, Ronald. *A Short history of progress*, Canongate, Edinburgh, 2005

Zimbardo, Butler and Wolfe. "Cooperative College examinations: More gain, less pain when students share information and grades", *The Journal of Experimental Education*, 2003, 7 (2), 101–125